A powerful and, indeed, magnificent portrayal of who Jesus is and what He meant us to be. You will love this book and love to share it with others.

RAVI K. ZACHARIAS, President,
Ravi Zacharias International Ministries

Jesus and the message of the Cross don't always bring "peace" but often cause a clash with contemporary "spiritual" philosophy. Joe Stowell has written a thought-provoking book that challenges Christians to shine as light in a post 9/11 world where the word. "God" is acceptable but "Jesus" is not.

PASTOR JIM CYMBALA,
The Brooklyn Tabernacle Church

Joe Stowell's latest book, The Trouble With Jesus, *is a compelling testimony to the pre-eminence of Jesus and a clear call to authentic Christian faith. In a post 9/11 world of new paganism and religious confusion, this is a message which begs to be read. I am so thankful for Dr. Stowell's willingness to share his bold heart and faithful witness. He is God's man with God's message for our times. This book is a life-changer!*

DR. JACK GRAHAM, Senior Pastor,
Prestonwood Baptist Church

THE TROUBLE WITH JESUS

JOSEPH M. STOWELL

MOODY PUBLISHERS
CHICAGO

All Scripture quotations, unless otherwise indicated, are taken from the *New American Standard Bible*®, Copyright © 1960, 1962, 1963, 1968, 1971, 1972, 1973, 1975, 1977, 1995 by The Lockman Foundation. Used by permission.

Scripture quotations marked NIV are taken from the *Holy Bible, New International Version*®. NIV®. Copyright © 1973, 1978, 1984 by International Bible Society. Used by permission of Zondervan Publishing House. All rights reserved.

Scripture quotations marked NLT are taken from the *Holy Bible, New Living Translation*, copyright © 1996. Used by permission of Tyndale House Publishers, Inc., Wheaton Illinois 60189, All rights reserved.

Scripture quotations marked NKJV are taken from the *New King James Version*. Copyright © 1982 by Thomas Nelson, Inc. Used by permission. All rights reserved.

Scripture quotations marked EMT are from *The Emphasized Bible*, by Joseph Bryant Rotherham (Grand Rapids: Kregel, 1959).

Scripture quotations marked KJV are from the King James Version.

Library of Congress Cataloging-in-Publication Data

Stowell, Joseph M.
    The trouble with Jesus / Joseph Stowell.
        p. cm.
    Includes bibliographical references.
    ISBN 0-8024-1093-6
    1. Christianity--United States. 2. United States--Religion.
3. September 11 Terrorist Attacks, 2001--Religious aspects--
Christianity. I. Title.

BR515 .S755 2003
277.3´083--dc21

                                                    2002015414

1 3 5 7 9 10 8 6 4 2

Printed in the United States of America

*It is with deep appreciation that I dedicate
this book to my dear friend and colleague of many years*

Duane Litfin

*His love for Jesus and passionate defense of His Name
in both word and deed are a constant
encouragement and motivation to me.*

CONTENTS

WITH THANKS...

I am deeply indebted to many of my colleagues whose commitment to our Lord and His work have freed me to work on this manuscript...

- The Senior management team at Moody, who share the oversight of the ministry with me.
- My Executive Assistants, Lori Imhof and Sonja Larson, who organize my schedule and deal with the many details and responsibilities that pile up on my desk on a daily basis.
- Sonja Goppert, whose capable assistance in research and manuscript development made this book more than I could ever hope it would be.
- Dr. Bryan Litfin, for his helpful review of the manuscript.

- The good people at Moody Publishers, who shared the vision for this book and worked so hard to bring it to you . . . hats off to Greg Thornton, Anne Scherich, Dave DeWit, and Bill Thrasher.
- Most importantly, Martie, my wife and friend, whose careful review of the manuscript took the book to a much higher level.

As the Lord uses this book to sharpen your focus and ignite your passion to live effectively for Jesus, thank our Lord for these highly valued friends without whose help *The Trouble with Jesus* would have never made it to your hands.

Above and beyond all of these, the glory and credit is due to Jesus, who has chosen and called us to the high privilege of being His advocate in an increasingly hostile world. Without Him there would be no cause worth living for and no Savior worth writing about.

Peter writes of Jesus:

As you come to him, the living Stone—rejected by men
but chosen by God and precious to him—

you also, like living stones, are being built into a spiritual
house to be a holy priesthood, offering spiritual sacrifices
acceptable to God through Jesus Christ.

For in Scripture it says:

"See, I lay a stone in Zion,
a chosen and precious cornerstone,
and the one who trusts in him
will never be put to shame."

Now to you who believe, this stone is precious.
But to those who do not believe, "The stone the builders
rejected has become the capstone,"

and, "A stone that causes men to stumble and a rock that
makes them fall." They stumble because they disobey the
message—which is also what they were destined for.

But you are a chosen people, a royal priesthood,
a holy nation, a people belonging to God,
that you may declare the praises of him who called
you out of darkness into his wonderful light. . . .

Live such good lives among the pagans that,
though they accuse you of doing wrong, they may see
your good deeds and glorify God on the day he visits us.

1 Peter 2:4–9, 12

BREAKFAST WITHOUT JESUS
The Traditions That Divide Us

The Chicago Leadership Prayer Breakfast is an annual event held the first Friday after the week of Thanksgiving. If you work in Chicago, attending the breakfast is the religious thing to do, second only to showing up at church on Christmas and Easter. I have gone to the event for the last fifteen years.

I can remember years ago when the name of Jesus was freely used in prayers and sermons alike at the breakfast. And though that has been slowly changing, this year's event was marked by what seemed to be an intentional effort to eliminate references to Jesus from the platform. If it weren't for the marvelous music of the Wheaton College choirs, who unashamedly sang about Him, the whole morning would have drifted by without the mere mention of

His name. I doubt if the choirmaster had been required to submit the texts of the repertoire to screen them for references to Jesus, given what took place in the rest of the program.

The MC opened the early morning get-together by reading an excerpt from Diane Eck's best-seller, *A New Religious America: How a "Christian Country" Has Become the World's Most Religiously Diverse Nation.*[1] He then underscored that diversity of religion in America now demands a new paradigm regarding the expression of our faith. He called for a fresh wind of cooperation and tolerance. His words set the stage for all that was to follow.

A representative of Islam chanted his prayer in the name of Allah. A woman rabbi, a Catholic priest, and a minister from a characteristically liberal Protestant denomination each led in prayer in a coordinated sequence of prayers and then finished by praying in unison.

I kept waiting to hear it, but Jesus' name was not mentioned once.

No one said that He wasn't welcome, but the message was clear. All our "gods" are to be equal. And when that is the agenda, the authentic Jesus is trouble. It's difficult to include One who has claimed to be the *only* way to God when a diversity of paths to God is being celebrated.

What was unspoken in the symbolism of the prayers was made unmistakably plain in the message that followed. The rector of Trinity Church, Wall Street, New York City, was introduced as being deeply involved in the problems and ministries surrounding the disaster of September 11, 2001. I looked forward to what he had to say. He proved to be an excellent communicator, as he charmed us with his wit and well-timed humor. We were deeply moved as he related stories of tragedy and triumph at Ground Zero. However, as his message progressed, he put into words my worst fears about post-9/11 America.

In essence, he celebrated the fact that after September 11 a whole new sense of the importance of God had returned to America. As he put it, "Theology is the name of the game after 9/11!" But, he noted, given the broad diversity of religions in America, we now need to give up the "traditions" that divide those of us who believe in "God." He praised the diversity the prayer segment had expressed.

It was then that I began to realize why Jesus was unwelcome. He was telling us in no uncertain terms that an "Only-Way-Jesus" didn't fit in the new religious order.

I could have shrugged it off as an isolated voice out of touch with the rest of America if it weren't for the fact that this sentiment is being propagated broadly. *New York Times* columnist Thomas Freidman writes, "It is urgent that the different religions 'reinterpret' their traditions to embrace modernity and pluralism and to create space for secularism and alternative faiths."[2] In an article in the *Chicago Tribune,* Bishop C. Joseph Sprague of the United Methodist Church's Northern Illinois Conference echoed that sentiment when he said, "I am always fearful when we in the Christian community move beyond the rightful claim that Jesus is decisive for us, to the presupposition that non-Christians . . . are outside God's plan of salvation. That smacks of a kind of non-Jesus-like arrogance."[3]

Lamenting that many are so exclusive in their own traditions that they don't allow God to speak through other traditions, our speaker of the morning went on to say, "9/11 will help you and me let go of some things that keep us from realizing that God works through others." He then quoted our Chicago poet, Carl Sandburg, who reportedly said, "The worst word in the English language is 'exclusive.'" The speaker's intention was clear: No one should claim an exclusive corner on the pathway to God.

To push Jesus out of the picture because He is exclusive is not the whole story. As Anne Graham Lotz said on Moody Broadcasting's national program *Open Line,* "Jesus is the only way, but He is not exclusive. He welcomes all to His offer of eternal life. No one is excluded at the cross."

That morning I wish I could have proclaimed the good news that Jesus welcomes all who will come.

Asking for More Than I Can Give . . .

Having asked us to give up the traditions that divide us, it was clear that the "tradition" he was asking me to give up was *Jesus*.

In my mind it is a gross underselling of Jesus to call Him a tradition. But that is exactly what He was being called. If I would just be willing not to speak His name in public prayer or articulate His exclusive claims to deity, truth, or redemption, we could get on with the business of celebrating our plurality of gods. Or, if I would be willing to strip Him of His rightful claim to supremacy and re-engineer Him so that He could "get along" with other gods, everything would be fine.

Let's face it. While not exclusive in the wideness of His mercy, Jesus is exclusive in His claim that He is the only solution for our sin problem and the only way to God. And that indeed He *is* God. Jesus is the central issue that separates me from Hindus, Muslims, Jews, New Age adherents, and the advocates of any other form of religion. His claims are unique. Without shame He said, "I am the way, the truth and the life: no man cometh unto the Father, but by me" (John 14:6 KJV). The apostles didn't miss the point. They proclaimed without reservation, "There is no other name under heaven that has been given among men by which we must be saved" (Acts 4:12).

My friend Dr. Kent Hughes, pastor of College

Church in Wheaton, Illinois, says that in the Garden of Gethsemane Jesus agonized with His Father to be relieved of the torturous ordeal of the Cross. Jesus' plea was for His Father to design another way to get the work of redemption done. After all, given His divine, unlimited creativity, and infinite wisdom, God would have been the best one to craft an alternative plan. But there could be no other plan because the sin problem needed a Savior. And God, in the person of Jesus dying on the cross for our sins and defeating death through His resurrection was the only solution.

There is no other way!

JESUS ABOVE ALL OTHER GODS . . .

Merging Jesus into a meaningless equality with other "gods" flies in the face of His rightful claim of preeminence. Try to downsize Him after reading this list of unparalleled credentials:

Christ is the visible image of the invisible God. He existed before God made anything at all and is supreme over all creation. Christ is the one through whom God created everything in heaven and earth. He made the things we can see and the things we can't see—kings, kingdoms, rulers, and authorities. Everything has been created through him and for him. He existed before everything else began, and he holds all creation together.

> *Christ is the head of the church, which is his body. He is the first of all who will rise from the dead, so he is first in everything. For God in all his fullness was pleased to live in Christ, and by him God reconciled everything to himself. He made peace with everything in heaven and on earth by means of his blood on the cross.* (Colossians 1:15–20 NLT)

Make no mistake. Jesus is unequaled. He doesn't compete.

Every hope, every confidence, every ache in our soul demands Jesus as He claims to be.

As the breakfast talk continued, my mind raced down the road of what Christianity without Jesus would be like . . . of what my life would be like if I had to give Him up.

- *Without Him the story line of the Bible disappears. The whole of Scripture is about rectifying the fatal consequences of the Fall. The promise of the remedy; the nation that carried the seed; the birth, death, and resurrection of The Solution; and the assurance of ultimate eternal victory is what the Bible is about.*

- *Without Him my guilt remains and I have no hope of forgiveness.* "If we confess our sins, He is faithful and righteous to forgive us our sins and to cleanse us from all unrighteousness" (1 JOHN 1:9).

- *Without Him I can't get to God.* "There is one . . .

mediator between God and men, the man Christ Jesus"
(1 TIMOTHY 2:5 KJV). *In fact, my relationship to
God rises or falls on my attitude toward Jesus. As
Jesus Himself said, "He who does not honor the Son
does not honor the Father, who sent him" (John 5:23
NIV). It's simple. You can't have one without the other.*

- ***Without Him heaven is gone and hell remains my
  just reward.*** *"There is no other name under heaven
  given to men by which we must be saved"* (ACTS
  4:12 NIV).

- ***Without Him I don't have a prayer.*** *"You may ask
  me for anything in my name, and I will do it"*
  (JOHN 14:14 NIV).

- ***Without Him I have no joy.*** *"I have told you this so
  that my joy may be in you and that your joy may be
  complete"* (JOHN 15:11 NIV).

- ***Without Him I've lost my friend.*** *"I no longer call
  you servants, because a servant does not know his
  master's business. Instead, I have called you friends"*
  (JOHN 15:15 NIV).

- ***Without Him I've lost my guide.*** *"Follow Me!"*
  (MATTHEW 9:9).

- ***Without Him I've lost my eternity.*** *"But whoever
  drinks the water I give him will never thirst. Indeed,
  the water I give him will become in him a spring of
  water welling up to eternal life"* (JOHN 4:14 NIV).

"Whoever believes in the Son has eternal life, but whoever rejects the Son will not see life, for God's wrath remains on him" (JOHN 3:36 NIV).

So much is at stake!

I was being asked to give up the most valuable treasure of my life. My heart was saddened and unsettled. As a follower of Jesus, I was being told that there was no room for "my kind" and certainly no room for my Jesus in this new world order.

Those who know me best will tell you that I am anything but an alarmist. In fact, I am wired toward optimism to a fault. Yet on that December morning I couldn't shake the heaviness in my soul.

KEEP HIM TO YOURSELF . . .

To be fair, I am confident that advocates of this new religious diversity would readily say that Jesus is OK as long as you keep Him to yourself. After all, in our enlightened culture we are all entitled to our own opinions as long as they don't interfere with or offend the sensitivities of others.

In other words, you can keep Him, but keep Him to yourself.

Which begs the question. Can Jesus be a private thing, or did He come to announce to the whole world that He alone brings forgiveness, healing, and hope to an otherwise confused and eternally lost humanity?

Is it possible to embrace His claims privately and at the same time deny the broad public implications of His mission? Can He be valued in our songs of worship and the rhetoric of our sermons and then be set aside for a greater cultural cause?

No one in the early church had the impression that Jesus was a private affair. They were, in the words of historian Will Durant, like "offices of propaganda" spreading the word to every willing ear.

STICKING UP FOR JESUS . . .

I could have written off the whole speech as just another preacher gone soft. In fact, I kind of had that "Well, I'm not surprised to hear this from a liberal New York parish priest" feeling when my worst fears were realized.

As the rector concluded his remarks, I remember thinking, *I wonder how this crowd is going to respond?*

No sooner had the thought crossed my mind than the audience stood in enthusiastic, extended, thunderous applause.

I felt awkward. Awkward and alone.

For the first time in my life, I was being asked to publicly deny Jesus. By joining in the standing ovation I would affirm the speaker's premise that it was best for me to give up the "tradition" that divided us. It was clear. The only way I could stand would be to turn my back on Jesus.

People at tables all around me were on their feet in boisterous support.

Yet I knew I shouldn't stand. I felt unsettlingly conspicuous.

But as embarrassing as it was, I didn't stand. I couldn't. And I was sick at heart. Though saddened by what was being done to Jesus in the name of religion, I remembered that it wasn't the first time He had been rejected. And although those around me weren't crying, "Crucify him!" they were rooting for and celebrating a religious world without Jesus. The same Jesus who was sent by the religious crowd of His day to die outside the gates was being similarly dismissed in Chicago.

I kept thinking, *Maybe I'm overreacting. Making too much of a fleeting moment in time. Being too sensitive . . . too reactionary.* I would like that to have been the case. But my heart and head said no. In fact, my colleagues from Moody who were with me, but who couldn't see me because they were sitting in front of me, didn't stand either. The issue before us was that clear. Any thinking Christian would have felt the heat.

At that breakfast I made a decision. I committed myself to *stick up for Jesus* whenever and wherever . . . regardless. Though I knew that this decision might come at a cost, I was ready to take it on. Experiencing Him has been the pleasure of my life; now, sticking up for Jesus would be the privilege of my life. After all, He stuck up for me two thousand years ago on the cross at ultimate cost to Himself. Sticking up for Him was the least I could do.

Tell me that I am not alone.

What would you have done?

I can't imagine anyone of us who know and love Him who wouldn't say, "I'll gladly be His advocate, anytime, anywhere!"

THE UNEXPECTED CHANGE . . .

Although the claim was widely embraced that after 9/11 America would never be the same again, I had not expected this. While the speaker's sentiments about Jesus had been lurking under the cover of secularism for some time, they were now out of the closet and ruling the day. As I left the breakfast, I recalled the *Larry King Live* show a few days earlier when John MacArthur was drilled in the aftermath of September 11 about the singular claims of Christ —and how MacArthur's voice was marginalized by the other panelists. And I understood what Shawn Hannity of Fox News meant when he said to Anne Graham Lotz a couple of weeks later, "Are you saying that Jesus is the only way? You know how mad that makes people today, don't you!"

Gene Edward Veith observed in *World Magazine* that the day has now come when "faithful Christians better be ready to become unpopular. . . . To say that all religions are true means that no religion is true. The only way to bring them under one umbrella is to deny their distinctive teaching." In this environment, Veith said, "Christians will find themselves demonized as 'intolerant,' perhaps our culture's worst term of abuse." He concluded by asking this question: "Christians have endured martyrdom, but can they endure unpopularity?"[4]

Bright Lights . . .

A pastor in Connecticut recently told me that after closing his prayer, "In Jesus' name," at a town meeting, he was visited by several clergy requesting that he not use the name of Jesus publicly in the future. When he explained that he couldn't do that, they proceeded to take out ad space in the newspaper calling him "divisive," isolating him from the religious community of his town.

John Dooley pastors the Apostles Lutheran Church in Chesapeake, Virginia. He has been a leading advocate of bringing people in his area together for prayer and mutual support in advancing the cause of Christ. So it was no surprise that he was asked to participate in a community wide service that included a broad diversity of faiths in the area.

He was considering accepting the invitation until he saw the literature for the event, which announced, "We are all Children of God and have a place in God's Kingdom here and in heaven." Knowing that

Muslims, Hindus, and other non-Jesus faiths were being included, he could not in good conscience affirm that all those who were included in the event had "a place in God's Kingdom and in heaven." He graciously declined. It was not an easy decision. Pastor Dooley is not a belligerent person. In fact, he said, "had there been rioting against Muslims or anyone else I would have gladly stood with a Muslim cleric . . . even called him a friend, and definitely would have called for an end of violence."

The backlash against Pastor Dooley and other nonparticipants was swift and vicious. In an article in the "Issues of Faith" section of the local newspaper, *The Virginian-Pilot*, Betsy Wright wrote:

> Once again members of my faith have gotten their boxers in a bunch. . . . A handful of local pastors . . . are worried that interfaith prayer services diminish the Gospel message. . . . OK, boys, all together now, let's take a deep breath and r-e-l-a-x. . . . Interfaith prayer services do not diminish the Gospel message. On the contrary, I believe these events reinforce the heart of Jesus' teachings and allow Christians to share the gospel in a radical way.
>
> I know personally that my faith has been deepened and enriched by interfaith experiences, as has my love for God and all humanity.
>
> So how can any Christian denounce anything that helps a human keep the two commandments

that Jesus said were the most important of all: loving God and loving your neighbor?

... The answer is fear.

That's OK. Keep your fears, ye folk of little faith. But do us brave believers who know we can be in the world but not of the world a favor: stay home, lock yourselves away in your tiny, I've-got-God-in-a-box world.

Then lock your lips and throw the key away.[5]

The inference in this vitriolic attack was that Ms. Wright was on the side of Jesus and the Bible and that those who conscientiously declined to attend were the true deniers of the faith.

Nothing could be further from the truth!

Services that affirm the legitimacy of false religions by demonstrating that we are all one and praying to the same "god" do injury to the gospel message. Pastor Dooley was right not to cast his lot with an event that would keep Jesus out of bounds.

It would be hard to imagine the apostles getting together with synagogue leaders and priests of pagan temples to join in common prayer. The only interfaith service I know of in Scripture is the service where Elijah prayed to God in front of the prophets of Baal. The prayers of Baal's followers were of no avail, but in response to Elijah's prayers, God sent fire from heaven to ignite a water-drenched sacrifice, demonstrating that He alone is God (1 Kings 18:17–46).

We must never forget the First Commandment, which says, "You shall have no other gods before me" (Exodus 20:3–4).

JESUS IS THE ISSUE . . .

In a letter to Christian leaders, Bill Bright, founder of Campus Crusade, warned, "The reality of our position has never been more plain. Generally, secular news media allow the promotion of any religion. . . . It is fashionable to speak of Buddha, Mohammed, Confucius, but the name of Jesus is too often *persona non grata.* One can say nearly anything demeaning of a Christian. Recent comparisons of Biblical Christianity to the Taliban in Afganistan are merely the beginning . . . which, left unchallenged, will leave the next generation of Christians to be the most assailed in our history."

If Bill Bright is right, and I think he is, the defining issue for followers of Christ of our generation is, *What we are going to do with Jesus in a world that either doesn't want Him as He claims to be or wants to put its spin on Him to yield a harmless, sedate Jesus who threatens no one?*

Living for Jesus has never been more challenging!

DÉJÀ VU ALL OVER AGAIN
Jesus and the New Paganism

I'm not used to having my messages sabotaged by outbursts of objection, so you can imagine my shock when a man in the front row blurted, "No! You can't be right. If we don't get America back we have lost all hope." His objection was a response to my comment that, "given what has happened in the last fifty years, I doubt that we will ever go back to an America where God and His values rule our culture."

Not wishing to offend the gentleman, I mumbled a feeble transition and pressed ahead, hoping he wouldn't feel moved again!

Nine months after that front row interruption, the horrible events of September 11 unfolded. On the day after the terrorist attacks I found myself wondering if indeed the man voicing the objection had been right.

By all appearances America had made a remarkable about face.

After a decade of bitter animosity between politicians in Washington, the entire Congress, from those to the left of Barney Franks to those right of Attila the Hun, stood on the steps of the capitol for all the world to see and sang "God Bless America" with the gusto of a barroom chorus.

America's heroes were no longer highly paid athletes who quibbled over one more million in their contract. Instead, our admiration shifted to unsung firemen, policemen, doctors, nurses, and emergency personnel.

The New York Times reported that a poll reflected racial tensions melting in the aftermath of the disaster. Blacks and whites now viewed each other as fellow Americans.

Patriotism soared. Strains of "America the Beautiful" fell from our lips with increased passion and emotion. And, in my opinion, no one sang it more wonderfully than Ray Charles.

A sense of morality was back. The PC cops had not let us use the word *evil* for years, but now the terrorists reminded us that there really are some things that are clearly evil—and the word was back in our vocabulary again.

I got the sneaking suspicion that it was all right to pray again. It seemed that everyone was praying —from our president to schoolteachers to people walking the streets looking for lost loved ones. People who had never thought of prayer as a valid life option were pleading with others to pray and admitting to practicing prayer themselves.

And, most important, God was back. "God Bless America" was sung at the opening of nearly every public event with caps over hearts and tears in our eyes. Long ago banished to the far regions of irrelevance, He was now welcomed with unashamed fanfare.

The Day That Everything Changed . . .

If 9/11 proved nothing else, it proved that we are desperately in need of something bigger than ourselves. Something above and beyond ourselves. As the burning heat snuffed out the lives and fortunes of corporate power brokers . . . as massive clouds of dust and debris chased savvy, successful people down the street and around shelterless corners . . . we realized that in and of ourselves we couldn't cope. In spite of what we had said for many years, we really did need God.

Peter Berger notes that "catalytic experiences are . . . 'signals of transcendence' . . . an experience in our everyday world that appears to point to a higher reality beyond [and] punctures the adequacy of what we once believed while also rousing in us a longing for something surer and richer."[1]

Despite the tenacious grip of postmodern secularism on our nation, America was now gasping for breath with a sudden need for God. We need a transcendent reality to help us in a secular society that was unable to comfort or heal. We were free to speak God's name again. He was now welcome in the hearts of Americans and in halls of power.

I was thrilled that our president called the nation to prayer on the Friday after the terrorist attack. It was a remarkable moment. The previously cynical press embraced the event like eager altar boys. Dignitaries and beltway politicians lined the front rows like approving deacons and elders. The world watched as America paused to join the president in prayer.

"A Mighty Fortress Is Our God" was sung with power.

The president delivered a reverent yet moving message peppered with biblical references.

Not surprisingly, Catholics, Jews, Muslims, and others were well represented in the program. And although each of the representatives of the various faiths was allotted a few minutes to speak, Billy Graham was given the privilege of delivering the major address. Dr. Graham spoke of his faith in Jesus and pointed to the cross on the wall as he referred to the finished work of Christ.

Could it be that the front row protester had more faith than I? Was it possible that God had decided to ignite the revival in America that so many had fasted and prayed for? I could hardly contain my ecstasy at the thought that "just like that" we had gotten it all back.

At least that is what I thought.

Under the silver lining of the demise of secularism the signs of a new and troubling cloud began to emerge.

As I basked in the glow of the momentous cathedral service, a friend said to me, "Did you notice that when 'A Mighty Fortress' was sung they omitted the second stanza?" I hadn't, and quickly recalled the words.

> *Did we in our own strength confide,*
> *Our striving would be losing,*
> *Were not the right Man on our side,*
> *The Man of God's own choosing.*
> *Dost ask who that may be?*
> *Christ Jesus it is He;*
> *Lord Sabaoth, His name,*
> *From age to age the same,*
> *And He must win the battle.*

My bubble of enthusiasm began to deflate with the thought that they had omitted the reference to the supremacy of Christ in the battle against evil. Jesus and His victorious role in history against the adversary had apparently been deliberately excluded.

Why?

Growing up in church-world I have been in lots of services where we threw verses away on a regular basis. You know, those times when we only needed two of the four verses to get the choir out of the loft. But somehow I doubted this was what was going on.

Had the organizers not wanted to offend the Jewish participants? Or, was it the Muslim who spoke and led in prayer that they were trying to please? As noble as the intention may have been, the statement was clear. The thought of Jesus as "the Man of God's own choosing," as the supreme and exclusive victor over evil, was too disruptive. Too divisive.

It was becoming clear. In post-9/11 America, God was back but Jesus was not.

Which means that when we say that God is back, it is important to ask, "*Which* God?" The god of Islam? The god of Hinduism? The gods of the New Age? The God of Abraham, Isaac, and Jacob? Or, the God of Abraham, Isaac, Jacob, and their Seed, the promised Messiah called Jesus, who came to our planet to befriend and redeem a fallen race?

Saying that "God" is back in the mainstream of our national life really means that it is now respectable to celebrate many gods in America.

A NEW DAY DAWNS . . .

The secularism that we thought had dissolved in the heat of September 11 has instead been eclipsed by the emergence of an updated version of paganism.

Let me explain. Paganism describes a society that embraces a wide-open spirituality, with a multiplicity of gods and no central moral authority. The only rule that paganism jealously guards is that no one god has final and exclusive rights as the only true god. Paganism allows your god as a preference but never as *the* singularly preeminent God.

Waking up to the reality that paganism is the new religious configuration of our nation demands a shift in our thinking and a new strategy if we are to advance the cause of the One-and-Only-Jesus. When we lived under the cultural consensus of secularism, our stand for *morality* was constantly challenged. Because of our unflinching commitment to the biblical absolutes of right and wrong, we were viewed as *reactionary, oppressive,* and *dangerous.* Now, in our pagan culture, it is our *message,* the message of an "only way" Savior, that is challenged. If we dare to stick up for Jesus by affirming His claims, we are considered to be *arrogant, intolerant,* and *divisive.*

BACK TO THE FUTURE ...

Before you get too demoralized, let me hasten to remind you that throughout history God's work has often been carried out with great success in the midst of paganism. Abraham wandered among pagans so fanatic that they sacrificed their children to gods of wood and stone. Throughout the Old Testament, Israel was called to advance God's glory among pagan nations that threatened their existence. But the premier example of success in the midst of a hostile paganism is the story of faithful followers of Jesus in the first three centuries.

In fact, it is uncanny how the issues they faced are so parallel to ours. The prevailing view of religion in their day was that "god" existed as a generic notion of transcendent deity. Access to this god was through the worship of whatever god or gods you chose. There was no "one and only God." The refusal of followers of Jesus to buy into this system of religion explains why their detractors often called them "atheists." It was clear to everyone who paid attention that Jesus and His Father, did not fit among the gods of the empire.

In A.D. 170, the Greek philosopher Celsus wrote a major book detailing the beliefs of Christians. In it he noted, "If you taught them [the Christians] that Jesus is not [God's] Son, but that God is father of all, and that we really ought to worship him alone, they would no longer be willing to listen to you unless you included Jesus as well, who is the author of their sedition." In fact, Celsus went on to accuse the Christians of "serving two masters." Early church scholar Robert Wilken observes, "Christians had introduced a new feature . . . namely, the worship of a man, Jesus—and in giving adoration to Jesus, they had turned men and women away from true devotion to God."[2]

Sound familiar? Everyone today is happy to believe in a generic ultimate reality they call "God."

And, as the speaker at the Chicago Leadership Prayer Breakfast assured us, you can commune with this being through lots of different gods.

What a mistake!

C. S. Lewis confronted this misguided notion in his classic work, *The Chronicles of Narnia.* In the last story of Narnia, *The Last Battle,* the worship of the evil god Tash is forced upon the residents of Narnia. A lamb who is a follower of the lion Aslan, the Jesus figure in the story, protests. "Please, I can't understand. What have we to do with the Calormenes? We belong to Aslan. They belong to Tash. They have a god called Tash. They say he has four arms and the head of a vulture. They kill Men on his altar." The wicked Ape, who was planning the takeover of Narnia, deceptively replied,

> Tash is only another name for Aslan. All that old idea of us being right and the Calormenes being wrong is silly. We know better now. The Calormenes use different words but we all mean the same thing. Tash and Aslan are only two different words but we all mean the same thing. Tash and Aslan are only two different names for you know Who. That's why there can never be any quarrel between them. Get that into your heads, you stupid brutes. Tash is Aslan: Aslan is Tash.[3]

Then Lewis reminds us of the reality that over-shadows all the cheap anti-"Jesus is the only way" talk. At the end of the story, the evil Tash unexpectedly appears, having been summoned by a Calormene warrior who carelessly called upon a power he didn't truly believe in. But Tash had no power over the followers of Aslan, the Christ figure of the story. Aslan's loyal follower spoke to Tash, commanding, "Begone, Monster, and take your lawful prey to your own place: in the name of Aslan and Aslan's great Father the Emperor-over-sea."[4]

In the same way, the self-styled religious hype of Rome was unable to captivate the early followers of Jesus. It is noteworthy that in the midst of a pagan-ism not unlike the paganism dawning in our America today, early Christians gave birth to the new, radical revolutionary Jesus movement. And, I should add, they didn't wear T-shirts that said "I Survived Pagan-ism!" They did much more than survive. They thrived! And they did so in spite of the fact that their allegiance to the person and message of Jesus put them at great risk.

What They Were Up Against . . .

A brief glimpse into their plight will help us get a grip on how to succeed for Jesus in our day.

Every aspect of their lives was challenged by pa-ganism. Economically, socially, morally, and recreationally, the gods of their day permeated their entire culture. There wasn't a *shade* of secularism in the Roman Empire. There didn't need to be. Paganism at its best permits everybody to live as they please with the benefit of spirituality to soothe away any thought of guilt or shame. Cohabitating with male or female prostitutes in the temples, as an act of worship demonstrates the point.

Paganism was so rampant in Ephesus that the mayor, or, as they called him, the clerk of Ephesus, was required as a part of his civic duties to offer a sacrifice publicly to a different god every day of the year.

All the trades had guilds which included both employees and management. Each guild had its own god to whom it looked for prosperity and protection. At each gathering of the guild, the patron god was worshiped and appealed to for direction and success. If you refused to bow, you were ostracized. And, after all, who would shop at your roadside stand once word got out about your refusal to comply? No one would want to fan the flame of his god's anger by associating with you, a "god-denier".

The baths, which were the centers of social interaction and recreation, were steeped in worship of the gods. Business deals were struck in the baths, and friendships were made and maintained there. You couldn't fully participate without bowing to the gods that lined the walls of the baths. In fact, you would be considered odd and on the margin of the community if you abstained.

The gods were amoral or, more often, immoral, granting their adherents license for unrestrained sensual fulfillment. The preeminent goddess of the first century was Artemis, who represented virginity and motherhood. Her temples were filled with prostitutes who serviced her followers on demand. Since the transition from virginity to motherhood was consummated in intercourse, the act was celebrated as an act of worship and an expression of loyalty to the goddess. Believers who lived pure and chaste lives were disdained. After all, who would want to worship a god like theirs? A god so limiting and oppressive?

Now you can understand why the first wave of followers were so marginalized. Because of their loyalty to Jesus as "the only way," they were challenged in every aspect of their lives.

THE TROUBLE WITH FOLLOWING JESUS . . .

When Jesus is in trouble, faithful followers are in trouble too.

One of the leading reasons for the suffering of the early Christians was their refusal to proclaim, "Caesar is lord." This oath was a requirement in many parts of the empire and, it should be added, a unifying factor in a diverse collection of cultures.

But Christians and their offspring refused to join the happy chorus of Caesar worship. *Jesus* was their Lord. They would not deny Him by giving to Caesar what rightfully belonged to Him—their singular allegiance and love.

The fact that Christians refused to declare, "Caesar is lord," caused the church to be seen as a hotbed of subversives who posed a threat to the unity of the empire. The unwillingness of early Christians to "go along" eventually brought the wrath of the empire down on their heads. But the resolve of His followers could not be intimidated by the smell of burning flesh or the gleam of a blood-stained sword.

Christians in the Empire were the objects of damaging rumors and innuendo. Their primary allegiance to Jesus and each other as brothers and sisters in Christ over any other earthly bond brought the oft-repeated charge that they were antifamily. Since their communion dinners were called "love feasts," these events were widely rumored to be orgies and cannibalistic in nature since Christians "drank the blood and ate the flesh" of Jesus.

Their world did everything possible to paint them as the bad guys. It's no wonder that Peter told early followers to keep their behavior excellent in a world that slandered them as "evildoers" (1 Peter 2:12).

Yet, even in death and marginalization, these early followers engaged their world with a power that could not be quenched. Because of their fearless attention to living well in the face of these pressures, they eventually won the day, not by the sword but by their unflinching allegiance to the person and mission of Jesus.

The question for us is whether you and I will live in such a way that our lives will etch a similar legacy for the advance of Jesus in the mind-set of our neo-paganistic culture. We must not fail to address this issue personally and corporately.

We have much to learn from the early followers of Jesus. They give us hope. They show us the way and inject into our lives the serum of confidence and undaunted courage regardless. If you are seeking to be a devoted follower of Jesus in this non-Jesus world; if you desire to impact your world with the good news that only Jesus brings, then early Christians are your kind of people . . . or should I say, we should be *their* kind of people.

If you think you can't relate to them because you see them as simplistic people in a primitive world who would have no understanding of the pressing realities of life in our high-tech digitized world, think again. Our worlds may be vastly different but the terms of engagement are the same.

HOW SHALL WE THEN LIVE? . . .

Thankfully, Jesus did not leave us to grope through the darkness without a plan. Those first Christians who knew Him well understood what to do. They were not confused. The strategy was clear.

In the face of a hostile environment, the early Christians remembered what Jesus had taught them:

> *Blessed are you when people insult you and persecute you, and falsely say all kinds of evil against you because of Me. Rejoice and be glad, for your reward in heaven is great; for in the same way they persecuted the prophets who were before you.*
>
> *You are the salt of the earth; but if the salt has become tasteless, how can it be made salty again? It is no longer good for anything, except to be thrown out and trampled under foot by men.*
>
> *You are the light of the world. A city set on a hill cannot be hidden; nor does anyone light a lamp and put it under a basket, but on the lampstand, and it gives light to all who are in the house. Let your light shine before men in such a way that they may see your good works, and glorify your Father who is in heaven.* (Matthew 5:11–16)

This commission given to early followers has not changed. It is our strategy, our only hope to advance the glory of His name. It is the template for how we advance the cause of Jesus in our non-Jesus world.

TERMS OF ENGAGEMENT
Salt and Light in Action

S everal weeks after September 11, 2001, John MacArthur was invited to appear on *Larry King Live* to discuss how a loving God could permit the atrocities of 9/11. Rabbi Harold Kushner; Deepak Chopra, a spiritualist from California; and Dr. Hathout, a scholar of Islam and senior adviser to the Muslim Public Affairs Council, were also members of the panel. At one point, Larry King turned to Dr. MacArthur and asked him if he believed that Jesus is the only way to God and that those who reject Him are not going to heaven. John's answer was biblical and forthright. But in the face of Larry King's pointed questions and the inclusive perspectives of the other panelists, his views were quickly discarded.

As I watched how challenging it was for John to

verbally defend the fact that Jesus is the only way, I was reminded of how effectively Lisa Beamer had drawn the attention of the same interviewer to the value of Jesus just two weeks earlier. It wasn't that Dr. MacArthur bungled the opportunity. He didn't. It's just tough to "talk" the theology of Jesus into a world that despises His claims.

Whether Lisa knew it or not, she was "light" in one of the darkest seasons of grief and confusion in the history of our nation.

Her husband had become a hero of major proportions when he sacrificed his life to avert a fourth plane from victimizing another target on that crisp September morning. Left alone with two small boys and pregnant with her third child, she captured the attention of America with her unusual strength and poise in the midst of such devastating circumstances.

It was just days after 9/11 when she made her first of several appearances on *Larry King Live!* Speaking of her husband's role on that tragic day, she told Larry King,

He called the GTE airphone operator about 9:45 in the morning and started reporting to her what was going on in the plane, including that there were hijackers and they had taken over the cockpit and possibly killed the crew.

He was sitting in the back of the plane with 27 others, and he was sitting next to a flight attendant, perhaps Mrs. Lyles I'm not sure. But the plane began to fly erratically, and he was aware that this was a situation that was not a normal hijacking situation, and he informed the operator that he knew that he was not going to make it out of this.

His next response was to ask her to say the Lord's Prayer with him, and then he asked Jesus to help him. And once he got that guidance, he asked her to contact me—gave her my name and phone number and my children's names—and to tell us how much he loved us.

And then once he had all that business squared away, he did what Todd would normally do, and he took some action, and what he did was he told the operator that he and some other people on the flight were deciding to jump on the hijacker with the bomb. . . .

Larry King: Were you surprised at anything Todd did?

Lisa: No. . . . He was a man of action and a man of thought, and he would think through decisions before he made them, and he would seek wise counsel.

I think he sought wise counsel, certainly in calling on Jesus and saying the Lord's Prayer and getting his heart right. . . . And after he sought that wise counsel, he was ready to take action. And that was the way he lived his life, based on faith and action, and that's the way he ended his life as well. . . .

Larry King: You're not surprised, then, at the prayer either?

Lisa: Not at all. Todd, like I said, was a man of faith. He knew that this life was not all there is, and this life was just here to prepare him for his eternity in heaven with God and with Jesus. And Todd made sure every day that he did his best. He wasn't perfect, and neither am I. But he did his best to make sure that he was living a life that was pleasing to God and that would help him know God better, and he acted on that all the way to the end, and I'm so proud.

Larry King: You have two sons, David is three, Drew is one, and you're expecting a third child in January.

Lisa: That's correct. And people sometimes look at me, I think, and wonder, is she in shock, is she, you know, unrealistic about what the situation is, and they don't see me all the other times when I'm, you know, breaking down and losing my composure. But, certainly, the faith that I have is like Todd's, and it's helping me understand the bigger picture here and that God's justice will ultimately prevail and that we have more to look forward to than just what we see here around us on earth.

Larry King's facial expression and riveted attention made it clear that at this point he was unusually moved. And it was his concluding remarks that proved the power of Lisa's unflinching trust in Jesus . . .

Larry King: I admire your faith and your courage. You've given a lot of people a lot of hope here tonight. You're an extraordinary lady, Lisa, and we wish you luck, and we hope to see you again soon.[1]

Count on it, having interviewed thousands of people through the years, his words were not just polite expressions of condolence. He was deeply touched.

Jesus showed up in strength that night on national television. On the platform of great personal tragedy, the kind that would normally overwhelm non-Jesus people with deep despair and hopelessness, Lisa proved that Jesus works even in the worst of times. The "good-works" of unflinching trust and confidence caught the attention of a watching world. Good theology is often expressed best in action and attitude.

In Jesus' terms, it was *salt and light* in action. Lisa had engaged a hostile society with the *salt and light* of her life.

SALTING A FLAT AND TASTELESS WORLD . . .

Cracking the code of what it means to be salt is not difficult. When Jesus says, "If the salt has lost its savor," He underscores the reality that salt has the power to make a difference. In the ancient world salt was used to flavor, preserve, and purify. In Jesus' world, just mentioning salt would have meant that He was talking about something of great value. In fact, soldiers and others in Christ's day were often paid in salt—which explains the old saying, "He's not worth his salt."

As a flavor enhancer, salt adds zest and brings taste to what would otherwise be bland and disappointing. I love the metaphor. Salting our world means we are to avoid being grumpy, stagnated, out of date, and stodgy. We tend toward that at times. Unfortunately, soon after Christianity became the accepted religion of the Roman Empire something got lost in the victory. After observing Christians, Emperor Julian lamented, "Have you looked at these Christians closely? Hollow-eyed, pale-cheeked, flat-breasted, they brood their lives away unspurred by ambition. The sun shines for them, but they don't see it. The earth offers them its fullness, but they desire it not. All their desire is to renounce and suffer that they may come to die."[2]

The American editor, cynic, and libertarian, H.L. Mencken, once observed, "The chief charge of Protestantism to human thought is its massive proof that God is a bore"[3]

God help us!

As a friend of mine says, "If you have joy inside, you should have your heart telephone your face and let it know. "

What would your world look like if you were salting it?

As salt we should season our world with the celebrant, confident, optimistic, and joyous nature of our position and privileges in Jesus. Because of all we have in Jesus, life is rich and free. By contrast, ultimately, life without Jesus is hollow, tasteless, and an empty pursuit. Our mission is to engage a world that has gone flat on itself with the zest and added value that Jesus brings to life.

Relationships will be blessed when salty followers are present. No one should laugh more deeply, listen more intently, prove that life is worth living more forthrightly, than we who follow Jesus. When fallen lives intersect ours, they should sense the depth of joy and purpose that only Jesus brings.

Not only do we advance the cause of Jesus by

flavoring our world with His presence, but, like salt, we act as preservers as well. The drift toward decadence should be checked because followers of Jesus are present. Being salt means that we are better citizens who influence public policy, sit on school boards, occupy judicial benches, vote regularly, and speak out humbly yet clearly about morality and justice.

Our place of employment should be a better place because we are there encouraging our colleagues and putting in an honest day's work. People should trust us more because we are always true to our word. People should sense that there can be purpose and hope in life because they see it in us.

Followers who are keen on engaging their world with the salt of their lives measure their success in these terms. If you are truly salt, your family, friends, neighbors, and colleagues will feel that their lives are safer, purer, more protected against evil, and a little brighter because you are there.

How do you score?

The better you score, the more interested others will be in hearing what you have to say about Jesus, the source of your "salt."

Lighting the Night . . .

Light, on the other hand reveals, enlightens, guides, illuminates, and clarifies. Light is consistently victorious over the darkness. When Jesus said that light is like a city set on a hill that cannot be hidden, He underscored the fact that light is unique, observable, and penetrates the darkness.

When Jesus said, "In the same way, let your light shine before men that they may see your good deeds and praise your Father in heaven" (Matthew 5:16 NIV), He was making it clear that lighting our night is not about our words or our conformity to rules and traditions. It is about the good deeds that extend the love of Jesus in tangible ways to those in need around our lives. The true light is a life-related reality that non-Jesus people actually experience.

Light-bearers put skin on the claims of Jesus and show a watching world what God is really like.

Lighting Your Night . . .

How will you know when you are lighting your world? When there is something so unique and observable about the way you live that you catch the attention of a watching world! Your compelling and attractive life will snag the curiosity of others, who will wonder, *What is that they have that is missing in my life?*

You will know you are lighting up your world

- *when you are no longer satisfied to simply be light within the four walls of your home or church;*

- *when you engage your world with intentional, some-times sacrificial, and concrete acts of love that meet the needs of people you come in contact with;*

- *when your life remains uncompromised, so that the uniqueness of Jesus is never muddled or confused with the darkness;*

- *when your life so reflects the glory of God that others join you in living to glorify Him as well.*

Lighting your night is about having a life so well lived that it is hard to deny the validity of what you say about Jesus and His claims.

In an earlier book I reflected on the power of a light-filled life clearly exhibited at the Presidential Prayer Breakfast in Washington, D.C. Mother Teresa was the speaker. She made her way feebly to the rostrum over which her bent posture made her difficult to see. Seated to her right were Vice President Gore and his wife, while to her left, on the other side of the podium, sat President Clinton and the First Lady. In front of these who had tried to use the power of the highest offices in our land to strengthen the cause of abortion, she said:

I feel that the greatest destroyer of peace today is abortion, because it is war against the child, a direct killing of the innocent child, murder by the mother herself. . . .

By abortion the mother does not learn to love, but kills even her own child to solve her problems.

And, by abortion, the father is told that he does not have to take any responsibility at all for the child he has brought into the world. That father is likely to put other women into the same trouble. So abortion just leads to more abortion.

Any country that accepts abortion is not teaching its people to love, but to use any violence to get what they want. This is why the greatest destroyer of love and peace is abortion.[4]

The crowd rose to its feet in applause while the Clintons and the Gores sat in silence throughout the thunderous ovation.

As President Clinton rose to address the group, he said of Mother Teresa, "It's hard to argue with a life so well lived." The world's most powerful advocate of abortion had little to say in the face of a life characterized by the compelling outcomes of good works. While I have some theological differences with Mother Teresa, I must say that my heart rejoiced at the power of her compelling acts of righteousness. Her words carried more weight as a result of her good works.

Is there anything about your life that is so well lived that others find that your consistent good works validate your words about Jesus? Lighting your non-Jesus world is about having a life that is "so well lived"!

OUT OF THE SHAKER . . .
OUT FROM UNDER THE BUSHEL!

What we cannot miss is that both salt and light are only effective when they engage their surroundings. Salt left in the shaker is of no use. In fact, Jesus reminds us, if it is left to itself for too long, it loses its potency and there is no hope for it to regain its use. And light is of no use when it is covered up.

We have no choice but to accept the challenge of salting and lighting our world.

I wonder if we are really ready to embrace this agenda. For too long, American Christianity has not engaged our world. It has been primarily about us. Our best-sellers are consistently books on how to enhance our personal relationship with Christ; how to solve our family problems and money woes; how to study the Bible and glean deeper truths; how to build bigger and better churches; and how to pray more often and with greater power. Aside from a periodic best-seller by Chuck Colson or Ravi Zacharius, there are comparatively few books that push us beyond ourselves to the commission of Jesus to engage our world.

I need to be clear here. Slow down and absorb what I am about to say. It needs to sink to the depths of your consciousness in a soulish way. This call to salt and light our world insists that we get beyond ourselves and our cloisters and intentionally connect with our world on His behalf.

This point cannot be taken lightly. Comprehending its vast, profound ramifications lays claim to the entirety of our lives and will catapult us beyond the petty issues, personal preferences, and gripes that so often derail us.

Getting Beyond Ourselves . . .

She stood in line long after the service to talk to me. I could see her coming out of the corner of my eye and knew that she had something urgent on her mind. She did. At least it was urgent to her.

She and her husband were thinking about leaving the church. When I asked why, she rather sanctimoniously informed me that their pastor had joined a country club. I happen to know the pastor well. He serves a very large and growing church and lives with all the typical stresses that go with that kind of calling. He is an avid golfer and finds that the brief seasons of getting away "to visit the Greens" are therapeutic for him. She went on to stack the deck against him by saying that her husband had found many verses in the Bible that proved her pastor was biblically wrong (I doubted it, but didn't challenge her on that point). To top it off, a neighbor told her that the pastor in question had been seen having brunch at the club with his family the previous Sunday morning. And, she said rather indignantly, "Why wasn't he in church?" Well, the church where he is the pastor has a Saturday night service. Since he was on vacation at the time, and knowing him, it's my guess that he went to church the evening before.

I mentioned to the concerned woman that the church was doing a splendid job of impacting its community for Jesus and that the test of a worthy church is probably decided on a different plane than where the pastor plays golf. I encouraged her to raise her perspectives to the higher issues of advancing Christ in our world. In fact I suggested that we should be pleased that such an articulate follower of Jesus could take the light to club members who need Jesus. She replied that Jesus would have taken His light to the streets, to those in poverty and despair. She totally ignored the reality that Jesus' love also covers country club golfers who stand in need of His grace.

The conversation is typical of the kind of insipid, downgraded, embarrassing stuff that occurs when followers forget we are called to the task of getting beyond ourselves and engaging our world. When church is only about us and our preferences we invariably implode on ourselves.

Getting serious about engaging our world means that we need to mark the pitfalls that so often disable advocates for Jesus.

Assimilation . . .

One challenge is the problem of becoming assimilated into the world. The early church often struggled with losing its uniqueness and becoming too much like its environment. As you probably know, the problem with the Christians in Corinth was that there was too much of Corinth in the Christians. In our day as well, assimilation threatens to take the punch out of our saltiness. Jesus warned that we might become so lax that our salt loses its flavor and becomes useless. Salt without flavor forecasts the danger of our becoming just like the world in which we live! In other words, from Jesus' point of view, we add no value to our world. Countless numbers of us are like that. Aside from the fact that we go to church and keep a few particular rules, others would never know the difference. We gossip, complain, and otherwise sin with the best of them. Be warned . . . assimilation is an ever-present danger. As someone well said, "If you were accused of being a Christian would there be enough evidence to convict you?"

Isolation . . .

Jesus also warns that light can be rendered of no effect by our isolation. His warning that we dare not put the light under a bushel was a clear signal that He knew our tendency to betray the light by shielding it from those who need it most. And His command that we let it shine "before men" so that "they may see your good works" distinctly defines our lives as light that refuses to exist in isolation. Beware of the comfortable confines of disconnected Christianity— of small groups, choirs, commitees, and the business of His work in church world. His work is to take the Light of the World to our world. Don't be confused.

When Jesus called His disciples to salt and light their world, the really "good people" were anything but engaged with their world. In fact, they actually felt quite good about their disengagement. Their disconnect would have been articulately defended as "true religion." Which only raises a huge caution flag. Feeling good about how you do as a Christian is no guarantee that Jesus is pleased.

A quick look at the "good people" of Jesus' day helps us to take note of disabling pitfalls. As you read about them, do not confine them to the box of history. See if there is anything of "you" in their shortcomings. They shamelessly lived out their disengagement and isolation in four distinct ways.

CLOISTERING . . .

The Essenes totally withdrew from society and gave their lives to the preservation of Scripture. They lived in tightly bound communities with no contact to the outside world and particularly no contact with the hostile paganism of their day. Their report card for engaging the culture? "F"!

In fact, they were so disengaged they believed that no one who was lame, blind, or otherwise maimed would qualify to enter the kingdom. Their laws of purity would not allow it. We could be highly critical of this approach if it weren't for the fact that many of us who call ourselves by His name are just about this disengaged. We know very few unbelievers. We stay in our safe, comfortable clusters and resist opportunities to interact with our pagan world. We pass on office parties. Invitations to dinners or events where we may feel a little uncomfortable are often refused. Our neighbors see little of us because we find it easier to spend more time at church and with our "friends" than we do engaging the guy next door. It's hard to be effective as light when you spend most of your time in the lighthouse with lightkeepers.

CORRECTNESS . . .

Unlike the Essenes, the Pharisees lived in communities that were well mixed with Jews and Gentiles. They had many opportunities to turn on the lights. Unfortunately, they kept flipping the wrong switch. For them, the most important way to let their light shine was to create a community identity based on keeping the rules. They had, as you probably know, all the rules, codes, and traditions down to a habit and were the 24-7-365 behavior police. Their intent was to be known by their rules and their strict adherence to them.

Rules were a means whereby they maintained Jewish identity. Good Jews obeyed the rules. Bad people didn't. It was just as simple as that. This all-consuming attitude separated them from the world they were called to engage. Tax collectors, sinners, and prostitutes found no door of mercy or grace through which to pass. Philo observes that the Pharisees were "full of zeal for the laws, strictest guardians of the ancestral traditions . . . who have their eyes upon transgressors and are merciless to those who subvert the laws."[5]

The Pharisees were violently opposed to Jesus for many reasons. High on the list was that while honoring the "real rules" He refused to give in to the oppressive rules that elevated the traditions of the Pharisees above the needs of people. Jesus was so dedicated to salting and lighting His world that He often engaged the bad people of His day on their turf. He defined "the light" as much more than a code of rules. The light was for those bound in darkness, and Jesus relentlessly illuminated those who needed it most.

It irritated the Pharisees to no end that Jesus lived a celebrant kind of life; feasting and dining with all kinds of people, while they practiced fasting, self-denial, and separation from sinners—the attitudes and behavior they wrongfully thought defined true spirituality.

If you are wondering if there is a parallel . . . think carefully. For generations, we have tended to elevate "rule-keeping" to the extent that it became the primary test of true-blue followers. Some of our rules were not then, nor are they now, explicitly biblical. Instead, they are, at times, man-made restrictions crafted to cover all the contingencies of living in a dark world so that earnest Christians are kept from getting too close to danger. The problem with these "extended" rules is that they isolate us from engaging a world that desperately needs our light. When we don't understand our true mission, we easily believe that conformity to church expectations is more important than engaging our world.

Don't get me wrong, righteousness is vitally important and "real rules" are indispensable. But they are not the primary means by which we engage our world. Our connecting identity is that we are Jesus' people who intentionally engage the world with the reality of His love and truth.

We would do well to identify those codes, traditions, and preferences that inhibit our capacity to relate effectively to non-Jesus friends, family, and neighbors. It's important to ask ourselves if the prohibitions that keep us from engaging are clearly biblical or are more a matter of tradition and preference. If they are not unmistakably demanded in Scripture, then they may at times need to be set aside if they get in the way of the greater good of relating biblically to those around us.

The issues will differ for all of us. I remember talking with a student who wondered if it was right to go to the bar with the guys he worked with. He had been trying to build significant relationships with them but realized that the relationships were developed after work at the local watering hole. I know of individuals who minister to gays and as a part of that ministry find that the neediest are often hanging out in gay bars. Should they go and find them there? What should you do if your neighbors finally ask you over for dinner and offer you a glass of wine as an act of hospitality? Or what should you do with the bottle of wine they bring over as a gift of appreciation when you ask them over for an evening in your home?

Would you miss church to go fishing with your colleague at work? Should you dance with your new daughter-in-law at your son's wedding when the MC calls the new father-in-law for the next dance? Should unchurched attendees at the reception be given the opportunity to wonder why you would refuse the normal courtesy of the next dance? Or, what should you do if when playing golf with three non-believing friends, they want to play for a small amount of "prize money" on each hole?

What message will we bring to the nonbelieving world? Will it be the message of our preferences and traditions or the liberating, lightbearing message of Jesus as Savior and Lord?

Granted, engaging our world will challenge our values and beliefs. Temptations are greater, discernment more necessary, and life is generally less predictable. Life is easier inside the salt shaker and far less challenging underneath the bushel. But the moment we get serious about engaging our world in effective ways for Jesus' sake, the risks get higher and neatly packaged answers disappear. Not everyone will understand and you may take some heat from your own troops. But the issue is critical. In what ways can you connect with the lives around you and still keep a clear conscience and pure heart? Jesus scandalized His religious world because He hung out with all the wrong people. But, as He said, He came to seek and to save that which was lost.

As one New Testament scholar has observed, Jesus fell out with the Pharisees precisely because His "kingdom-agenda for Israel demanded that Israel leave off her frantic and paranoid self-defense, reinforced as it now was by the ancestral codes, and embrace instead the vocation to be the light of the world, the salt of the earth."[6]

CONFRONTATION . . .

The Zealots fell into the third trap of disengagement. They were singularly focused on the overthrow of the Roman occupation. The freedom fighters of their day, they were ready to engage the pagan Romans at a moment's notice. If they were here today, they would probably wear fatigues with a Star of David proudly displayed on the shoulder. The Roman occupation was not to be tolerated, and all of them were willing to spill their blood in the streets for the cause. They were dedicated to restoring Israel to its rightful place of independence and honor through sharpened sword wielded in righteous determination.

In our day, bombers of abortion clinics would qualify as modern day Zealots, as would all the rest of us who are just flat-out mad about the sin and rebellion that goes unchecked in our culture. I have felt for a long time that the church in America is far better at venting our consternation than we are at practicing compassion and caring for the lost souls of the "occupiers."

Noticing the rapid slouch toward Gomorrah, we have spoken angry words, pointed self-righteous fingers, and written fiery volumes against purveyors of decline. The whining and grumbling index registers dangerously high when we talk about having lost our precious America. Don't get me wrong. I agree with the bumper sticker that says, "If you're not outraged you're not paying attention!" But we are to be among those who have learned to be angry without sinning and who don't let the sun go down on our wrath. In fact, the mark of our followership is that we love our enemies (Matthew 5:43–48).

I fear that we have embarrassed ourselves and betrayed the heart of God by being so long on mad and so short on mercy. With our spirits in a snit, we have often appeared to our world as just another irritated subgroup demanding our way with raised fists.

Let's admit it, Jesus had a better plan for engaging a dark and dying world.

Interestingly enough, the compelling person and message of Jesus captured the heart of one of these street warriors and transitioned his focus from violence to a message of engagement; from anger and war to a message of peace, mercy, and love. His name was Simon the Zealot. He is listed among the twelve disciples.

It is important to note in the ministry of Jesus that while He was clear about sin and repentance, He never expressed anger toward the pagans in the environment. When He expressed His anger it was reserved for religious folk who oppressed God's people with their greed and burdensome rules. It was the hypocrisy of religious leaders and their distortion of true godliness that ignited the wrath of Jesus—a thought well worth a moment of reflection for those of us who consider ourselves "good people" with "appropriate" disdain for a decadent culture.

As true followers we are to be salt and light, not an angry mob.

COMPROMISE . . .

Lastly, the Herodians and the chief priests engaged their world, but did it through compromise and acquiescence to the power structure of that day. Herod could only enjoy temporal power and prosperity as long as he cooperated with Rome. The chief priests—the leaders of the synagogue—held their lucrative positions with the blessings of Rome. They gained everything they wanted but in the process had lost their capacity to be salt and light.

Countless numbers of modern-day Christians have not wanted to hibernate or to be bound by a multiplicity of rules. They have felt uncomfortable with those who always want to pick a fight with the world. Unfortunately these Christians have chosen to engage the world by embracing the world. Pleasures, self-satisfaction, and material comforts dominate their agenda. Life is more about their cars and clubs than about the good works that emanate from a unique reflection of the character and purity of Jesus. These Herodian types rarely think "kingdom" thoughts and live as though this is the only world there is. The radical calling of Jesus rarely registers even though they are regular churchgoers and would classify themselves among the better people of our world.

DON'T MISS THE POINT . . .

It should not go unnoticed that Israel's great mistake was to assume that the pagan world around them was a target for the imminent judgment of God. Without that in mind, the thought of engaging their world with the light and glory of God was simply not on their spiritual radar screen. However, through the Old Testament and into the time of Jesus, God's will was that Israel would glorify Him among the pagans. He never intended that they withdraw from their world and wait for its destruction. As a result of their failure to carry out God's plan, His judgment fell not on the Roman Empire but on Israel. In A.D. 70 Jerusalem was demolished in a devastating attack. They had failed in their mission to light their world by engaging it with God's power and grace. N. T. Wright notes, "God's purpose would not after all be to vindicate Israel as a nation against the pagan hordes. . . . On the contrary, Jesus announced, increasingly clearly, that God's judgment would not fall on the surrounding nations, but on the Israel that had failed to be the light of the world."[6]

We dare not be content to sing the old gospel song, "This world is not my home, I'm just a' passin' through," as we anticipate with detached interest His judgment on our world. Jesus was anything but detached from His world. He cut a swath of salt and light that the world could not ignore. Christ brought the salt and life of His life to a needy culture even when it meant He had to die to accomplish the task.

When I was a boy in Sunday school we often sang, "This Little Light of Mine." One stanza went, "Hide it under a bushel?" at which point we would shout as loud as we could, "No! I'm going to let it shine." As the Scripture says, "A little child shall lead them" (Isaiah 11:6 KJV)! Amen!

The early church didn't miss the point. They effectively engaged their world with the salt and light of what they said and did. Their lives and community efforts were lived out in at least "five ways" that are all appropriately transferable to our lives. These five commitments shape the game plan for how we can make a strategic difference for Jesus in our pagan non-Jesus world.

Commitment number one in our quest to "stick up for Jesus" is a willingness to "speak up for Jesus" in clear and convincing tones.

CHAPTER 4

JESUS IN THE NO-SPIN ZONE

Commitment 1:

Declaration . . . Speaking Up for Jesus

Martie and I had escaped to the countryside of England to do some writing and recover from the hectic pace of our existence. We felt wonderfully far away and it was easy to forget the Chicago Leadership Prayer Breakfast of a few weeks earlier. It was Christmas Eve and I had an hour or so before we were leaving for the midnight Christmas Eve service at the village church. I grabbed the December 24 edition of *The Times,* London's leading newspaper, and plopped onto the sofa to catch up on the news. When I got to the editorial page, I noticed a bold headline: "The Nativity Is a Scandal and Should Remain One." I braced myself for another attack on the Jesus of Christmas and began reading:

September 11, as NASA told astronauts on the Endeavor shuttle, was "not a very good day down here on Earth." Seared for ever on the minds of all are the apocalyptic images of breathtaking hatred and inconceivable malice. And the word that had been all but banished in our new millennium was suddenly common parlance: evil.

Religion took centre stage. Millions, especially in America, streamed into churches for solace and for answers. As the American Civil Liberties Union looked on in despair, Americans were singing with gusto God Bless America and plastering In God We Trust on every available billboard. Pundits even began predicting a religious revival in the West. One thing seemed certain: Post-Modernism was dead: suffocating political correctness was passé.

However, political expediency soon rendered that assessment naively premature. . . . Quite simply, the need to maintain a united front against the terrorists and to avoid a clash of civilisations meant that this was not the time for exclusive religious claims, but for tolerance and ecumenism. . . .

And into this context comes Christmas. With the PC brigade more active than ever, we should not be surprised that this season the baby Jesus is being presented in even more bland and innocuous terms than in previous years. . . . For in the current environment even the baby Jesus is a potential victim of the spin-doctors.

The fact is that we miss the whole point of the Christmas story if we try to make the infant Jesus fit our agenda rather than acquiescing to His agenda. For this Jesus would not forever remain the meek and mild baby: according to Gabriel He would be 'great', perfectly 'holy', the unique Son of God, the Jewish Messiah, the one and only saviour of humanity. Try as we might, to reduce the Nativity to a symbol of generic human love and peace among persons of differing belief, it simply does not work, because essential to the Christmas story are claims concerning who the child is—unsettling, necessarily offensive claims to ancients and moderns alike. From conception to the grave the controversial Jesus scandalised people, and thinking human beings will continue to be affronted by His radical, divisive mission, which climaxed in His death on the Cross . . . and which mandates from us a decision, whether of faith or cynicism. PC, anaesthetised readings of the Christmas story are just damnable, despicable distortions of God's most significant intervention in human history.

At this point I am on the edge of the sofa, hardly believing what I was reading on the editorial page of a global newspaper. Could it be that an editorialist somewhere on the other end of a computer keyboard had decided that it was about time to stick up for Jesus?

He concluded:

> This Christmas let us not insult the Christ child
> by attempting to tame Him for our causes, recruit
> Him for our campaigns, or use Him to promote a
> flaky PC agenda. Don't get me wrong: the infant of
> the Nativity scene does indeed come as a message
> of love, peace and goodwill from God, but only on
> His terms, which subvert human logic and tran-
> scend political spin. I don't know about you, but I
> find the Nativity to be one of the most delightfully
> subversive, refreshingly offensive, and shockingly
> scandalous events in all of human history.[1]

Needless to say, I was stunned by the clarity of
this no-holds-barred statement, written into the teeth
of our post-9/11 spin-Jesus world. Wondering who
would have written such a clear and pungent proclamation, I looked at the byline and was wonderfully
surprised to note that it was my friend and Moody
graduate, Colin Nicholl, who at that time was on
the divinity faculty at Cambridge University.

CLARITY OF MESSAGE . . .

I couldn't have gotten a better Christmas present.
I loved every word of the article. It had the ring of
the bold proclamations of the early church. Have no
doubt about it. Those who knew the salt-light strategy

best, knew that a clear articulation of the essential truths about Jesus was indispensible when it came to informing the darkness about what must be believed to be truly Christian. While the London *Times* is not the platform for a new Pentecost, the clarity and directness of Colin's words reminded me of Peter's forthright declaration of the gospel when he fearlessly confronted celebrants at the Jewish feast of Pentecost. Without flinching, the Peter who denied Jesus over a charcoal fire now declared:

> *Men of Israel, listen to these words: Jesus the Nazarene, a man attested to you by God with miracles and wonders and signs which God performed through Him in your midst, just as you yourselves know—this Man, delivered over by the predetermined plan and foreknowledge of God, you nailed to a cross by the hands of godless men and put Him to death. But God raised Him up again, putting an end to the agony of death, since it was impossible for Him to be held in its power. . . .*
>
> *Therefore let all the house of Israel know for certain that God has made Him both Lord and Christ—this Jesus whom you crucified.* (Acts 2:22–24, 36)

The sermon set the template for the proclamation of the gospel. Man was guilty. Jesus was victorious over sin and death. Through the Resurrection He was undeniably affirmed as Lord and God. Nothing short of full repentance was the only way to remediate the insolvable dilemma of our alienation and guilt. And *only* Jesus provided eternal forgiveness and the gift of the indwelling Holy Spirit (Acts 2:38).

It was good news, and for early followers it was the *only* news.

And what was undeniably good news for pilgrims at the Jerusalem Passover event was also important news for heady philosophers in Athens. With the archsymbol of paganism, the Acropolis, as a backdrop, Paul engaged a group of intellects on Mars Hill with these definitive words:

> *Men of Athens, I observe that you are very religious in all respects. For while I was passing through and examining the objects of your worship, I also found an altar with this inscription, "TO AN UNKNOWN GOD." Therefore what you worship in ignorance, this I proclaim to you. The God who made the world and all things in it, since He is Lord of heaven and earth, does not dwell in temples made with hands; nor is He served by human hands, as though He needed anything, since He Himself gives to all people life and breath and all things. . . .*
>
> *Therefore having overlooked the times of ignorance, God is now declaring to men that all people everywhere should repent, because He has fixed a day in which He will judge the world in righteousness through a Man whom He has appointed, having furnished proof to all men by raising Him from the dead.* (Acts 17:22–25, 30–31)

There wasn't an inch of wiggle room in the early church's soul or speech when it came to the reality of who Jesus was and what He claimed to be. Jesus defined His mission and message at a meeting of insiders in the Upper Room, when He claimed—without equivocation—to be *the* way, *the* truth and *the* life. And then added, "No one comes to the Father except through me" (John 14:6 NIV). He proceeded to validate that claim by paving the way to God by becoming the only risen sacrifice for sin. Early followers unashamedly embraced the proposition and fearlessly proclaimed it as soul-binding truth. In fact, they were so successful that before long they were known to friend and foe alike as people of "the Way" (Acts 9:2 NIV; also NASB).

If we are to succeed, we too must keep the message clear and plain. Particularly because so many are trying to transform Him into the image of their own agendas.

JESUS IN THE SPIN ZONE . . .

To hear Rosie O'Donnell talk you'd hardly believe that Jesus is on the "outs" in America. In fact, we hear His name spoken of frequently in admiring and embracing ways. It seems as though everyone wants Jesus in their parade. From gay activists to abortionists to religious leaders to politicians, making Jesus fit their agendas and flying His flag provides a guise of propriety and credibility.

Rosie recently outed herself as an avowed lesbian. Her first major crusade was to promote the adoption of children by gay parents. One testy news anchor talked her into one of the few interviews she granted after coming out of the closet. During the interview she talked about the deep agony of her growing up years. She spoke of her new life as a liberating and satisfying replacement for the abuse of her past. I watched with great interest and utter amazement as the conversation continued.

The skilled, and obviously religiously savvy host, referring to the now-retracted statements from some religious leaders that 9/11 was partially caused by gays in America, asked Miss O'Donnell if she felt threatened by that sort of rhetoric. Her response was shocking. Basically, she said no, since she more than anyone understood the teachings of Jesus . . . namely, love, kindness, compassion and understanding. When the intrigued interviewer pressed O'Donnell on whether she risked ultimate judgment from God because of her lifestyle, she calmly replied, "No." Her reason? After all she had endured in her life, she felt convinced Jesus would smile on the fact that she could love at all.

As I sat silent, I thought to myself, "Jesus was being spun big time." He is either the Righteous One who will judge everyone according to their works, or He is Rosie's Jesus who tolerantly and lovingly embraces her life choices regardless.

THE 9/11 SPIN MACHINE ...

The war on terror triggered a phenomenon that only added to the confusion about the authentic Jesus.

As Colin Nicholl has noted, soon after that horrible day in September, it became evident that it was politically necessary, for the sake of not alienating Arab nations we needed in the war against terror, to present Islam as a religion of peace and good will. Our president took great pains to make the point both in public proclamations as well as in visits to several mosques. In a strange way, the September attack on America has become a PR coup for Islam. It is now mainstreamed alongside of Christianity and Judaism as a major player on the field of religion in America. This has enabled us to put another god into the mix of gods already on the god shelf of our emerging paganism. Islam, unlike Judaism, reveres Jesus; but like Judaism, it denies His unique claims, which only muddies the waters in terms of public perception.

In the midst of this effort to legitimize Islam, a church in the Chicago area invited a Muslim to speak about his religion. The well-intentioned effort was staged to help followers of Christ understand that not all Muslims are hateful murderers and to engender an ongoing Christlike love for Muslim people. In the course of the interview the Islamic devotee was speaking of the many similarities between Islam and Christianity. He said, "All of us, you believe in Jesus, I believe in Jesus. I believe in Muhamud and all the prophets. So our mission is to introduce people to God."

Not really.

Muslims believe that Jesus was a prophet of the highest order, but they do not believe that He is God, as He Himself claimed to be. They deny that He was born of a virgin. They deny that He rose from the dead. And they reject the fact that His death was the final and ultimate atonement for sin.

There is no way that they believe in Jesus like we do. Not the real Jesus. It was pure spin. But then "Jesus" gives Islam credibility—especially in America —so let's make Him fit.

But making Jesus fit is a problem. For Him to fit, you have to twist and disfigure Jesus in serious ways. In order to become all things to all people, Jesus must be spun as not having said what the Bible affirms He said. A one-size-fits-all Jesus must be tolerant of everyone, judgmental toward none, kind but not analytical, loving but not disciplining, a moldable figment of every imagination, a bland, almost boring, toothless, inoffensive, nondivisive, disposable Jesus.

It is our responsibility to keep Jesus in the no-spin zone by speaking up for Him on a regular basis at appropriate times and in appropriate ways.

JESUS IN THE NO-SPIN ZONE . . .

Early followers of Jesus kept the message clear, and some paid with their lives for the privilege. Given the price they paid, the least we can do is speak up for Jesus as well, regardless of the cost.

In times like these, knowing *what to do* begins with knowing *what is true about Jesus* and making sure that there is not the slightest erosion. We must know that He is God, as He claimed to be. That He is the only way. That His death on Calvary finished the work of salvation. That all who come, apart from any work or merit and regardless of class, culture, or color, will be welcomed as His child. That He rose from the dead as final proof that He had conquered death and sin and hell. That He is coming again. That He will judge the world.

The doctrines of the early church stood in bold contrast to the pagan options offered to the average citizen of the empire. Interestingly, the exclusivity of Jesus as the only way became an attractive element, given the broad array of options that all the gods and goddesses provided. Into a world where massive numbers of deities often left their adherents confused and unsettled, Jesus offered the clarity of being the one and only way. The matter was settled, and His resurrection had authenticated the claim. As one student of the early church observes, "There were too many cults, too many mysteries, too many philosophies of life to choose from: you could pile one religious insurance on another yet not feel safe. Christianity made a clean sweep . . . one choice, one irrevocable choice and the road to salvation was clear."[2]

The Resurrection also convinced believers that Jesus had defeated and reigned supreme over even the most evil of demons. The world of the gods of the first three centuries was filled with haunting fears of the arbitrary moods and ways of evil spirits. Jesus had conquered death and evil. Only His followers were free.

The Roman Empire was obsessed with the afterlife. Cultic priests and philosophers of the likes of Plato, Seneca, and Plutarch wrote and often speculated about issues of ultimate destiny. Jesus came from a real heaven, and He returned there in the sight of witnesses. The early church offered a certain destiny in Jesus. Jesus Himself promised to come and take all who believed in Him back to heaven (John 14:1–6). The debate was over. The terms were simple to understand, and the privilege was offered to all, regardless.

The early church remained faithful to the unique message of Jesus. They kept it clear, uncluttered, and understandable. It was a message molded by

God to satisfy the deepest longings and to stay the most unsettling fears and uncertainties. God had come in the person of Jesus to meet the real needs of real people who without Him are bound and deceived by false gods crafted to destroy them.

Don't miss the point! What we have to say to a watching world is good news. Really good news. God cared enough for us to come in the form of Jesus. As John wrote, He "pitched his tent" among us (John 1:14 ENT) to rescue us from the insolvable dilemmas of life as we know it. He proved time and again that He was indeed God. Amazingly, He died in our place for our sins to forgive and cleanse us. He rose the third day to guarantee victory over evil and hell. And He is in heaven this very moment advocating for His followers as He prepares a place for all who call on His name. He is coming again to take His followers home and to justly judge the living and the dead.

Keep the message clear. Your friends, family, colleagues, and neighbors who are caught in the web of modern paganism desperately need the news. Many are confused by gods of sensuality, power, materialism, and self-indulgence. They are disappointed by empty promises and lack of fulfillment. Others are worried about evil and its effect on them and their families. Experiencing a troubled, often nasty world, people around you need to hear that this is not the only world, but that Jesus has promised a "far better" world to come.

Speak the truth.

Speak it often. Speak it in humble, compassionate, and winsome tones. Speak wisely and patiently in ways that honor Jesus, and fairly engage the paganism of our day.

Speak it in appropriate moments. Speak it prayerfully. Speak it to your own heart. Speak it on planes, busses, and trains. Speak it to your children. Speak it fearlessly.

But speak it.

The message of Jesus is the "power of God unto salvation" to all those who repentantly follow Him (Romans 1:16 KJV).

In a world like ours, with its multiplicity of gods and a wide-open spirituality, it is actually quite fashionable to talk about "god" and to admit that some needs cannot be met in purely material or intellectual ways.

I have mentioned this before in other writings, but to be honest I don't know of anyone who spoke more clearly to the longing of hearts for the satisfaction that only Jesus can give than Douglas Coupland. Coupland is a best-selling author of books about life and society in post-Christian America. Here is what he said in his *New York Times* bestseller, *Life After God:*

Now—here is my secret: I tell it to you with an openness of heart that I doubt I shall ever achieve again, so I pray that you are in a quiet room as you hear these words. My secret is that I need God—that I am sick and can no longer make it alone. I need God to help me give, because I no longer seem to be capable of giving; to help me be kind, as I no longer seem capable of kindness; to help me love, as I seem beyond being able to love.[3]

There are "Douglas Couplands" all around you who down deep are dissatisfied with the hollow ring of life and the charade that the empty promises have played in their soul.

Jesus is the answer.

Embracing and being willing to articulate the clarity of the authentic Jesus is an important part of getting your salt out of the shaker and your light un-busheled.

When No One Wants to Hear . . .

But I hasten to add that speaking up for Jesus may not always be the place to start when engaging our world. Watching John McArthur speak the truth about Jesus as the only way that evening on *Larry King Live!* reminded me again of how difficult it is to "speak Jesus" into the face of a culture that wants Jesus spun to its own terms.

Our words about God's Word are rarely what initially draws the hearts of would-be followers to Jesus. And while it is forever true that "faith comes by hearing, and hearing by the word of God" (Romans 10:17 NKJV), it is also true that getting your average pagan to hear what he doesn't want to hear is a major challenge. It is in the face of this challenge that salt and light, according to Jesus' terms, are dispensed—not only through our words but most importantly in our deeds.

Think of how difficult it is to tell a friend or colleague at work that he needs Jesus because Jesus is the only way to God. You'll inevitably hear questions like, "Are you telling me that good Muslims or Hindus are going to go to hell? What about those who have never heard?" It wouldn't be unusual to hear, "I thought that God was a loving God. If He is like that, I don't want to have anything to do with Him." Or, worse yet, you might hear, "You Christians are so arrogant! Who do you think you are to think you have a corner on truth? You're so intolerant."

But in spite of the inevitable resistance to the truth about Jesus, the salt and light strategy understands that while those around our lives may not be willing to hear what we have to say, they will be watching how we live. More closely than you might like to imagine. And when Jesus asks us to be the light of our world, He makes it clear that it is what unbelievers see in us and know about us that paves the way for us to speak on His behalf.

Which may be what St. Francis of Assisi had in mind when he quipped, "Preach the Gospel every day and when necessary use words!"

Or, to put it another way, there are times that before we can effectively *speak up* for Jesus we may need to light our world by first *showing up* for Jesus.

JESUS IN THE SPOTLIGHT

Commitment 2:

Demonstration ... Showing Up for Jesus

In the musical *My Fair Lady,* Eliza Doolittle, the soon-to-be converted to high society cockney street woman, cries in desperation for her beloved to not only tell her of his love but to show her. For her, words were not enough.

For years, most of us have thought that if we could engage a non-follower of Jesus in a meaningful conversation we would stand a pretty good chance of getting them to listen to us and perhaps even win them to Jesus. My father and grandfather preached into a culture that shared a basic intellectual acceptance to the claims of Jesus. People in their churches found that witnessing for Jesus at work or in their neighborhood at least had the advantage of a general cultural awareness of God, Jesus, sin, heaven, and hell. In their world hostility to the gospel was much more subdued. In those days people were more willing to listen to truths about Jesus and His claims.

For us it is different. As Dorothy said to her dog in the *Wizard of Oz,* "Toto, I don't think we're in Kansas anymore." Taking Jesus to the hearts of a needy world is more complicated in our times. The resistance is more intense.

In fact, in our culture words themselves get lost in the meaningless maze of "whatever it means to you is fine." Gene Veith, in his insightful work, *Postmodern Times,* tells this story about the difficulty of verbal witness into the postmodern mind-set:

> Charles Colson tells a story about a dinner he had with a media personality, and trying to talk with him about Christianity. Colson shared with him that he needed to come to Christ. "Obviously Jesus worked for you," his friend replied, but went on to tell him about someone he knew whose life had been turned around by New Age spirituality. "Crystals, channeling—it worked for her. Just like your Jesus."
>
> Colson tried to explain the difference, but got nowhere. He raised the issue of death and afterlife, but his friend did not believe in Heaven or Hell and was not particularly bothered by the prospect of dying.
>
> Colson explained what the Bible said, but his friend did not believe in the Bible or any other spiritual authority.

Finally, Colson mentioned a Woody Allen movie, *Crimes and Misdemeanors,* about a killer who silences his conscience by concluding that life is nothing more than the survival of the fittest. The friend became thoughtful. Colson followed with examples from Tolstoy and C. S. Lewis on the reality of the moral law. The friend was following him. Then Colson cited the epistle of Romans on human inability to keep the law. His friend then paid close attention to the message of Christ's atoning work on the cross.

Although the friend did not become a Christian, Colson felt that he finally had broken through at least some of his defenses. The difficulty was in finding a common frame of reference. Because of his friend's mind-set, the usual evangelistic approaches didn't work. "My experiences," says Colson, "is a sobering illustration of how resistant the modern mind has become to the Christian message. And it raises some serious questions about the effectiveness of traditional evangelistic methods in our age. For the spirit of the age is changing more quickly than many of us realize."[1]

Which brings us to this crucial question: How can you engage a world where very few are ready to come to grips with what you have to say? Especially if you know little about Woody Allen, Tolstoy, or C. S. Lewis?

This is not to say that speaking up for Jesus is not critically important. We have just learned how important it is. The point is that while speaking up for Jesus keeps the definitions clear and the issues in play, it is *showing up* for Jesus in the way we live that has the power to attract the curiosity of a watching world and to break up the hardpan soil of their hearts.

THAT "WAY ABOUT YOU" LOOK . . .

Recently I received an e-mail from a new follower of Jesus who is learning how to live for Jesus in her non-Jesus world. She wrote,

I'm a relatively new Christian (6 months) . . . I was moved to tears at what you said. Since I became a Christian in the middle of the school year, it was very awkward for me, because my friends didn't understand all of the GREAT things that Jesus was doing in my life. I practically didn't understand either, but I was at peace, and I was ready to begin that walk as a Christian. It was actually my Senior year math teacher, Michelle, that brought me to Harvest for the first time, and I've gone ever since and was saved shortly after that first time.

Your message today meant so much to me, because I have a hard time really speaking up about Jesus. I know that I've been given numerous chances (friends will ask me for advice on a problem, and I try to help them out as much as I can). It's after those chances that I realize that I had a GREAT opportunity to tell them that they can turn to God when times are rough, and that He is the way that you will and can overcome ANYthing. This message really gave me the confidence to do just that. After hearing so many stories about others trying to dodge Jesus and speaking of Him . . . I realized that I should be proud to say that I am a follower of Jesus Christ, and He alone is all that I need. I don't need what everyone else says that I need. I need Him.

I was also glad that you brought up the point that people can stop listening, but they don't stop watching. My teacher (the one who took me to Harvest) always had a "way about her." I could never figure out what it was . . . and now I know!!! I need to really live to have that "way about you" look for me as well!!!

When Jesus commissions us to be light in our world, He makes it clear that there is a power more compelling than our words, which is important for all of us who have grown up in a Christian culture that thinks of evangelism in terms of words and verbal formulas. As we have noted, Jesus defines "light" as *good works* and informs us that the power of the light is in what people *see* in our lives.

Since "good works" are a critically important

part of impacting our non-Jesus world, let's slow down a little and look closely at how you can penetrate the darkness around you with the marvelous light of Jesus expressed through the way you live.

GOOD FOR NOTHING . . .

You may be experiencing a surge of resistance when you hear another demand for good works in your life. Let me ease your pain. Any thought that the light is about a stifling, oppressive, legalistic, performance-based, rule-preeminent Christianity is not what Jesus had in mind.

For which I am personally glad.

Let me pause here to let you in on a secret. Sometimes I get tired of being good. Not tired of Jesus. Not tired of the work of the Spirit, just tired of having to be good. Having grown up a pastor's son and then being a pastor myself and now having served as president of a Christian college, I know what it's like to live in the fishbowl of expectations—always having to be good.

In my worst moments I'd like to do something to shock people. Nothing unrighteous and immoral—I am well aware of how destructive that would be—but something slightly outside the lines for a change. Fortunately, when these feelings get running too high, the Spirit tells me to relax and stay in the big picture of what is best in the long run. Nevertheless, we all know how burdensome and sometimes seemingly boring rules can be if they are kept simply because it is the thing "proper" Christians do.

Thankfully, being good is far more strategic than just doing "the proper thing."

Good for Something . . .

The Greeks had several words for "good" in their language. The two used most often in the New Testament are *agathos* and *kalos*. *Agathos* generally refers to good in the sense of being morally upright. A respectable, honest person who lives within biblical boundaries is *agathos*. Growing Christians should be increasingly *agathos* in every area of life. But not just to be good for goodness' sake.

There are a multitude of reasons why we must be good (*agathos*) as followers of Christ.

In Psalm 1 it is clear that delighting in God's law and meditating in it day and night leads to a blessed life. Indeed! A blessed life is a life without haunting guilt, fear, loss of self-esteem, and all the other destructive baggage sin produces. It's no wonder that in Psalm 19:7–10 the psalmist revels in the fact that the law of God restores the soul and the testimonies of the Lord make the simple wise. He reminds us that the fear of the Lord makes us clean and the judgments of the Lord are true. So taken is he with the benefits and blessings of the "good life," that he exclaims of God's laws: "They are more desirable than gold, yes, than much fine gold; sweeter also than honey and the drippings of the honeycomb."

Goodness of life also has value in that it brings pleasure to the One we love. Righteousness is a worship language that enables us to express to Jesus how much we love and adore Him.

Peter was aware of the protection that *agathos* brings to our lives when he warned, "I urge you . . . to abstain from fleshly lusts which wage war against the soul" (1 Peter 2:11). Sin patterns in our lives, whether public or private, leave our soul vulnerable to Satan's attack.

And that is no little matter. Your soul is the essence of who you are. It is where God meets you. It is where all of life is planned and programmed. For a Christian, it is a fortified stronghold of spiritual vitality. It is where you draw strength to serve and glorify God. There is no more important part of your being than your soul. It is the real you.

A life that rejects the call of goodness and gives in to the flesh lets the drawbridge down, permitting the Enemy to storm the gates and wage a war that, when successful, discourages, dismantles, and destroys the inner work of God in our lives. And although most of us apply enough discipline to maintain a proper appearance on the outside, the truth is that a life given over to its own out-of-bounds desires is a life where the soul has been plundered and pillaged and as such is void of spiritual power!

Most importantly, in the context of our commitment to engage our world with Jesus, being morally upright gives credibility to our claims as followers of Jesus. It builds a platform on which the good works of our lives can be seen without the accusation of hypocrisy clouding the view. Not only does hypocrisy in our lives bother God, it gives a watching world an excuse to reject Jesus.

If our lives are not morally consistent with what we claim to be good and true, there is no hope of catching the attention of those in our lives. They will be too turned off to notice. People everywhere are desperately searching for something that is real. Something they can believe in that is solid, true, and satisfying. They want something that works. If we betray what we say is true by denying it in our lives, they will look elsewhere.

On one occasion when defending a friend against the attack of a group of "do-gooders," Harry Truman said, "In times past he owned a bawdy house, a saloon and gambling establishment . . . but he's all man. I wonder who is worth more in the sight of the Lord, he or the sniveling church members who weep on Sunday, play with whores on Monday, drink on Tuesday, sell out to the Boss on Wednesday, repent about Friday and start over again on Sunday?"[2]

Don't dismiss the acidic comment as a typical "give-em-hell" Truman moment.

When Truman was a teenager, he had a job at the local drugstore in his hometown. As such he was privy to a lot of town chatter and had an inside view of the behavior of some of Independence's leading citizens. One of the memories Truman had of those early days were the times when certain folk came into the store and went behind the counter for a clandestine downing of gin. He remembered them getting their drinks and then sliding money across the counter for him to put into the till. Unfortunately, these stealth-imbibers were leading lights in the local church and, in fact, the founders of the local chapter of the Temperance Union.[3]

This sort of blatant hypocrisy disengages the power of any good works we might do. But beware of the hypocrisy that is more subtly expressed in our attitudes. Our Christianity too often comes off as rigid, snooty, self-serving arrogance.

As one author notes, Christianity is often "a refuge for smug hypocrites who preach love of neighbor but practice adoration of self, who revile riches in public while plundering their neighbors the rest of the week, and who extol charity, sexual restraint and self-sacrifice, but are loathe to practice these virtues themselves. These Christians pay lip service to the Gospel but never embrace its fundamental message."[4]

Not exactly what Jesus had in mind when He called us to be lights of the world.

But as important as *agathos* is, it is rarely a compelling feature in drawing others to Jesus. It supports our claim that morality counts and gives us credibility as being consistent and satisfied. But the truth remains that while your average pagan may respect you for your good behavior, he probably doesn't find a heavy dose of *agathos* real attractive for himself. Try telling your unsaved neighbor that if he becomes a Christian he could begin to tithe! He most likely is less than interested in regular church attendance. He may actually like getting a little drunk now and then. A brief overnight fling or a lie to get himself out of trouble are among the things he might not want to give up. Most pagans would like the freedom to swear now and then on the golf course and to snoop around on the Internet after hours. So while being *agathos* is vitally important for us, it is not the key to drawing the hearts of a watching world to Jesus.

Which brings us to the good works that *do* have the power to open hearts to the message of Jesus.

The Power of "Kalos" Christians . . .

When Jesus speaks of good works as the definition of our being the light of our world, *kalos* is the word that is used (Matthew 5:16).

Kalos is goodness in the sense of doing good things.

The word most often casts goodness in terms of what is excellent, attractive, powerful, helpful, admirable, or well done.

In the context of "light," *kalos* is doing things consistent with what Jesus would do. Even a casual reading of the Gospel of John reminds us that His good works aroused the curiosity of the multitudes and provided an opportunity to proclaim the good news of the kingdom.

In order to understand the impact of "*kalos* works," we need to put *kalos* and *agathos* in perspective. To be *agathos* means that if you walk down the street and pass the local porn shop you quicken your pace and look the other way. But if in the next block you see a shivering street person in front of a Starbucks begging for enough money to buy a cup of coffee, and you continue on your way without giving thought to his need, you have failed to be *kalos*. In fact, if your heart is not moved to pray for the spiritual needs of those in the porn shop whose lives are cascading into destruction, then you have failed to be *kalos* as well.

You could be the best rule-keeper in town, but if you cringe and cold-shoulder the well-pierced counter-culture person who comes into your church, you have failed to be *kalos*. *Kalos* may not require that you like everything about a person, but it does demand that you receive him as another sinner in need —much like yourself—who has come within the sound of the good news.

Agathos is about rules . . . *kalos* is about relationships.

Agathos behaves . . . *kalos* blesses others.

Agathos does what is right . . . *kalos* forgives those who don't. Without exception.

Agathos tithes . . . *kalos* gives above the tithe to those in need with no thought of receiving in return.

Agathos may not do what others at the office do . . . *kalos* keeps a keen eye out at the office for opportunities to express the love of Jesus to fellow workers.

Kalos lights your world with attention-getting works that arouse the curiosity of a watching world.

You can't "do" Jesus in your non-Jesus world without it.

Which explains why Peter, in a letter written to followers spread far and wide in the hostile and decadent pagan world of the Roman Empire, put the *kalos* principle into the heart of his strategy for living for Jesus in a non-Jesus world.

To the marginalized, suffering followers he said, "Keep your behavior excellent among the Gentiles, so that in the thing in which they slander you as evildoers, they may because of your good deeds [*kalos*], as they observe them, glorify God in the day of visitation" (1 Peter 2:12).

GOOD DEEDS AND BAD PRESS . . .

As Peter noted, the early believers were often slandered "as evildoers." As we have noted, the enemies of the followers of Jesus spread rumors that their communion dinners were orgies, and since it was known that in their communion ritual they drank the blood of Christ and ate His flesh, they were criticized as "cannibals." Because of their demand for uncompromised commitment to Jesus over all earthly allegiances, they were despised for being antifamily. They were also slandered as enemies of the state for refusing to claim, "Caesar is lord."

So, given their bad press, how could they ever take the good news past the threshold of their house churches?

They engaged their world with the light of the "*kalos*-power" of their good works.

A few verses earlier, Peter wrote that believers are to "proclaim the excellencies of Him who has called you out of darkness into His marvelous light" (v. 9). The proclamation of the excellencies of Christ, he explains three verses later, are the observable *kalos* works of our lives.

The word picture in this text is fabulous. We have been brought from our own darkness into His light. And being in His marvelous light, we are to show off what He is like to a watching world. It is as though we have been called from the darkness of the back stage of our sin and alienation from God into the spotlight of His grace. The curtain parts and it is now your turn to do your part in showing off the reality of Jesus.

Peter makes an interesting point about life in the spotlight. He notes that "spotlighting" is particularly effective with people who have come to the end of themselves. He notes in verse 12 that observers will come to glorify God in the day of their "visitation." This is a word that is often used of the judgment of God for sin. Most scholars agree that Peter is not referring here primarily to the final judgment but to the present judgment that people experience when they live life without Him. The Bible is clear—and life validates the point—that life lived in an immoral, godless way feels the guilt, brokenness, bankruptcy, despair, and hopelessness that life without God ultimately brings. It's like Douglas Coupland said. My secret is that I need God—that I am sick and can no longer make it alone. At this point, it's the reality of Jesus in the lives of people they know that strikes a chord of hope.

You know it's working when someone asks, "I've been watching your life. What is it that you have that I don't ever seem to be able to find?" And then we can say, "Let me tell you about Jesus."

Jesus in Real Time . . .

My friend Paul Eschelman, founder of *The Jesus Film* project, recently told me a riveting spotlight story.

He was meeting with a group of advertising executives from a major Hollywood film company. They were discussing global marketing strategies for a new release of *The Jesus Film.* The senior executive was a Jewish man who had an immense profile in the movie industry. After the meeting, the senior executive asked Paul if he had a moment to meet with him privately in his office. Paul was surprised and of course gladly complied.

As they sat down, the marketing mogul began telling Paul about his life. He and his wife had sometime ago gone through a very serious health problem with their child. One day he noticed their live-in housemaid kneeling in her room in prayer. Later, he asked what she was praying for. She replied, "Your child, that God might be gracious to heal her." She went on to say that she had been praying for the child for days. In fact, she added, she prayed for the whole family every day. The film marketer was deeply moved and asked if she would come to the door each morning and pray a blessing over him and his wife as they left for work.

A few months later, his wife became seriously ill with breast cancer. With his wife at death's door, he walked down the street to find consolation at his synagogue. Discovering that it was bingo night, he kept walking and found a church with its doors open. He went in and met the pastor in the sanctuary. Pouring out his grief, the pastor prayed with him and assured him of his concern.

The next morning, when he went to visit his wife in the hospital, the doctor turned to him and said, "I thought you were Jewish?"

"I am!"

"Oh" the doctor replied. "Then why was a pastor sitting and praying at your wife's bedside through most of the night?"

As Paul sat listening, deeply intrigued, the man then said, as tears filled his eyes, "Our maid passed away this week. And now I have no one to get me to God. Can you help me?"

Paul said, "Can I tell you about Jesus?" To which he replied, "Of course!"

Before Paul left the office, the powerful executive had prayed to receive Christ as his Savior.

I should hasten to add that spotlighting may not always turn out so well. Not everyone responded to the good works Jesus did. In fact, His good works only made His enemies more determined to extinguish His light. But though not all will respond, some will.

What I love about Paul's story is that it was the *kalos* power of the good works of two faithful followers that opened the door for an otherwise resistant heart to hear the good news of Jesus. God used two spotlight players to lead a non-Jesus person to the light. Nothing spectacular, just two ordinary people taking the opportunity to *kalos* their world.

A pastor friend of mine serves in a California town that is without doubt among the most culturally radical communities in America. As he says, "It makes Berkeley look like a Sunday school picnic." For instance, you can walk down the street and see posters announcing séances that help you get in touch with departed spirits, and seminars to help you learn how to cast a spell on your enemies. Needless to say, Christians have not been held in high esteem. In fact they were an outright despised minority. It was hard for churches to get planning permissions, building permits, or any other normal benefits from the town fathers.

My friend tells me of many Pastors' Fellowship meetings where the topic of conversation was consumed with how difficult ministry was in their town. Whining about the awful environment characterized their gatherings. Tired of the negative tone of the meetings, one pastor suggested they pray about how they might be able to reach their town in spite of the hostility.

Brilliant!

They decided to engage their community with the salt-and-light agenda.

AIDS is a huge problem in their area. One of the churches established a ministry to AIDS victims. Individuals in other churches with medical and compassion service backgrounds engaged the elderly to spotlight Christ's love to many who were dying lonely and rejected. Another church chose to minister to the homeless; another to single mothers; another to pregnant out of wedlock teens; and another to kids at risk. The stage was full of spotlighters.

And though it wasn't an overnight win, in time their seacoast town began to notice that the Jesus people were bringing healing and help. Town fathers and social agencies began to call on the churches for volunteers, advice, and support. The churches were looked on as a part of the solution to the problems that inevitably come from life without God. In the day of "visitation," followers of Jesus showed up and by their observable works of light began to win the hearts of their fiercest enemies. Today, although not everyone in town has become a follower, the once-cowering churches are growing with a fresh vibrancy. And now it's a lot easier to get building permits.

Beyond Church Walls . . .

A friend came to me recently and asked what I would do differently if I were to go back to the pastorate.

The answer came quickly.

I would want to revolutionize the "status quo" mind-set of those who claim to be faithful followers of Jesus. Most of us have thought that being a good Christian is about accepting Christ, embracing and defending sound doctrine, keeping the rules, and in our best moments cultivating a relationship with Jesus. And while all of this is vital, it's not the total package.

If I could pull up a chair beside you right now, I would want to look in your eyes and tell you how pivotally important my next words are. Listen carefully. Authentic Christianity is not just about keeping and protecting the faith and keeping the rules. It is even more than living to deepen your relationship with Jesus. *Authentic Christianity, the real deal, is about embracing all of these important elements and using them as a resource to actively and intentionally engage your world with acts of love that show off Jesus.*

Anything short of this is a denial of His intentions for those of us who follow Him. If we don't actively engage our world on His behalf, we have fallen short of following Him. For if you follow Him, He will ultimately take you right to the needs of those around you. It is obvious to even the most casual observer that He came to effectively engage His world, not to hibernate with His chosen few.

In fact, you and I are redeemed and heavenbound because of His passion to engage our needs in the face of great hostility. The least we can do, as a debt of love, is to go and do the same for others. That is exactly what He commissioned us to do when He said, "As the Father has sent me, I am sending you" (John 20:21 NIV).

If I had one more opportunity to shepherd a flock, my desire would be to equip and mobilize His followers to engage our community—through programs, personal relationships, and casual encounters —with the brilliance of His light. Church was never intended to be an exclusive club focused inward. In fact, some of the truest forms of Christianity—terms of engagement—are often expressed outside the context of church. Who was it that said so appropriately, "The church is one of the few organizations to exist for the benefit of its nonmembers as well as its members"?

Real Christians work to build relationships into which they can pour the *kalos* power of Jesus. We must take the love of Jesus to our neighbors, to the afflicted and the poor . . . to the needs of those you work with and to the stranger who happens to cross your path.

And when they ask you why you have blessed them, tell them Jesus sent you!

Carl Henry writes, "Can we take a holy initiative in history? Can we once more strike an apostolic stride? Can we put an ungodly world on the defensive again? Can we show men the folly of opposing Him who has already overcome the world, of rejecting fellowship with the coming King? Will we offer civilization a realistic option, or only a warning of impending doom? Will Christianity speak only to man's fears and frustrations, or will it also fill the vacuums in his heart and crown his longings for life at its best?"[5]

The answer must be yes.

Are you ready to change your mind about what it means to be an authentic follower of Jesus . . . to repent of a life focused on your own agendas and start the wonderful adventure of life lived according to His intentions? Will you join me in making a difference for Jesus in your world by committing your heart, energy, and resources to the power of taking *kalos* to needy hearts that cross your path every day?

Where and with whom will you start?

JESUS TO THE NEEDY

Commitment 3:
Compassion ... Reaching Out for Jesus

The statistics are astounding.

Most scholars who study early Christianity agree that at about A.D. 100 there were approximately 100,000 followers of Jesus. By A.D. 200 they identify nearly 1.5 million, and then by the year A.D. 300, some estimate that as high as 6 million claimed allegiance to the cause of Christ. In an empire of 60 million, the church made up 10 percent.[1] Think of it! One out of every ten citizens refused to claim that Caesar was lord at great risk to their own lives. That is how compelling Jesus had become through the lives of early followers.

The numerical growth swells in importance when you factor in the wholesale martyrdom of Christians and the rampant disease and frequent plagues that ravaged Rome's territory.

The rapid expansion of the Jesus movement stretched from North Africa to the British Isles to Turkey. There wasn't a region of the empire left untouched. In fact, by the fourth century, the life-transforming message of Jesus had reached all the way to the most prestigious palaces of the empire. Sophia, the mother of Emperor Constantine, became a convert and no doubt was influential in bringing her son to Jesus. He, in turn, declared Christianity the official religion of the empire.

As one scholar notes, "No other new cult anywhere nearly approached the same success."[2] Another remarks, "It is the comparative success of early Christianity that demands an explanation."[3]

Tomes of literature have been written to explain the phenomena of early Christianity and, interestingly, for the most part, all come to the same general conclusions. It was not so much their dogma, although the beliefs of the early Christians played a part, it was rather their lives and the way they engaged their hostile world that made the remarkable difference. They were just what Jesus wanted them to be.

Early church historian Dodds recognizes that the most important cause of the growth of the Jesus movement was not their ideology, but rather the *kalos* factor evident in many of the early Christian groups.[4] The types of good works most often mentioned by those who know the actions of early Christians well are *compassion* and *community*. While their undaunted *courage* proved the point of their commitment, and their *consecration* to the message offered others something significant to believe in, compassion and community drove early Christianity into the mainstream of life in the empire. These two commodities offered an attractive alternative and an undeniable picture of the love of Jesus. They were the fields upon which the power of Jesus was unleashed. In what was often a loveless, hedonistic world full of gods that didn't love or help, compassion and community met the longings of the human spirit.

COMPASSION . . .

In the second century, Saint Lawrence, a deacon in the early church and treasurer of the church's resources, was brought before the authorities and asked to hand over all the church's treasures to the government. To refuse meant certain death. He compliantly asked for eight days to gather the treasures of the church, at which time he promised to present them to the emperor's representative. On the eighth day he appeared and brought with him orphans, the poor, the lame, and widows in distress. Pointing to them, he told the authorities, "These are the treasures of the church!" For that reply, Lawrence was sentenced to death in the fire and not many days later was roasted on a spit over burning coals.

That moment captured not only the attitude of the early church but the heart of Jesus. Jesus taught them, "Come to Me, all who are weary and heavy-laden, and I will give you rest" (Matthew 11:28). In fact, Jesus authenticated His claim to messiahship by telling the inquisitive disciples of John the Baptist, "Go and report to John what you have seen and heard: the blind receive sight, the lame walk, the lepers are cleansed, and the deaf hear, the dead are raised up, the poor have the gospel preached to them" (Luke 7:22).

Jesus caught the attention of His hostile world by reaching out to those in distress. His ministry did not court the power brokers of His day, nor was it negotiated in halls of influence and political leverage. To the shock of the religious leaders, His compassion would extend not just to those in physical distress but to those in the distress of sin. He hung out with tax collectors (He even recruited one to join His enterprise), talked to an immoral Samaritan woman, and offered forgiveness and full acceptance to prostitutes. He dined with greedy businessmen like Zaccheus, who repeatedly overcharged his customers. The list of those He came to help is long and diverse. Religious folk were aghast! Which says a lot about the blindness of the hyperspiritual.

If you had a need, physical or spiritual, the Light of the World was there. Early followers had learned the lesson well.

They cared because Jesus cared. And it gave credibility and authenticity to their message.

COMPASSION IN ACTION . . .

To this day, two thousand years later, historians applaud the unprecedented *kalos* effect early Christians had in their world.

"The Roman Empire was no welfare state," writes John McManners, "and before Christian times in the West . . . care for the poor was rare."[5] Classical philosophy, adds Rodney Stark, "regarded mercy and pity as pathological emotional defects of character to be avoided by all rational men. Since mercy involves providing unearned help or relief, it was contrary to justice."[6]

Christianity turned this notion on its head. Whereas, for the most part, the poor were formerly thought of as victims of a cruel destiny, Christians were told that to look closely at the poor was to see the face of God.[7]

Their care for the needy is legendary.

They would often fast, not for their own gain or spiritual advantage, as we so often do, but rather to take the money they would have spent on groceries and give it to the poor. The early church father Hermas wrote, "On the day when you fast, take only bread and wine. Calculate the amount of feed you would have taken on other days, put aside the money you would have spent on it and give to the widow, the orphan or the poor." Origen of Alexandria said: "Let the poor man be provided with food from the self-denial of him who fasts."

Early bishops in the church were required to eat one meal each day with the poor.

Babies that were deformed, unwanted, or of the wrong sex were often discarded on the dung heaps outside city gates. It was the Christians who went to the dump to gather the unwanted babies. They nourished and reared them in their own homes.

The Christian writer Tertullian (c. A.D. 200), wrote, "It is our care of the helpless, our practice of loving kindness that brands us in the eyes of many of our opponents."

Nowhere were these compelling virtues more evident than during the great and devastating plagues that swept the empire.

In their book *Christianity on Trial,* Vincent Carroll and David Shiflett observe:

> Two epidemics helped Christianity expand its reach. The first took place in the second century and was known as the Plague of Galen. It claimed the lives of perhaps a quarter to a third of the Roman Empire's citizens. A century later another terrible epidemic killed as many as five thousand people a day in Rome alone. . . . Any pagan who could leave town when major epidemics struck quickly did so. This was, after all,

an age that had little understanding of the origins of diseases, but understood very well the wisdom of putting as much distance as possible between oneself and a stricken neighbor. The terror that epidemics unleashed was but indescribable. Dionysius, bishop of Alexandria, paints a heart-rending picture of the resulting stampede: The pagans "pushed the sufferers away and fled from their dearest, throwing them into the roads before they were dead and treating unburied corpses as dirt, hoping thereby to avert the spread and contagion of the fatal disease; but do what they might, they found it difficult to escape."

The Christians' response was different from their neighbors'. They tended to stand fast in the cities and nurse the stricken. Providing food, water and basic sanitation was not enough to save all of the diseased, by any means, and cost many Christians their lives. [Rodney] Stark notes that Dionysius spoke of these sacrifices in an Easter letter:

"Most of our brother Christians showed unbounded love and loyalty, never sparing themselves and thinking only of one another. Heedless of any danger, they took charge of the sick, attending to their every need and ministering to them in Christ, and with them departed this life serenely happy; for they were infected by others with the disease, drawing on themselves the sickness of their neighbors and cheerfully accepting their pains."

[Rodney] Stark believes this rudimentary care

may have cut the mortality rate by two-thirds or more. This left a number of surviving pagans in an interesting situation. Many who had been succored knew they owed their lives to their Christian nurses, but they also had a deeper matter to consider: How was it that these Christians were able to survive in greater numbers that anyone else? Did Christianity enjoy an endorsement from on high?[8]

And while it is true that early Christians solidly positioned themselves against "the casual practice of infanticide and the abandonment of unwanted babies, . . . [and] opposed the exploitation of children for erotic pleasure, elevated the status of women, [and] accepted and broadened the Jewish tradition of concern for the poor,"[9] it is clear that they did more than preach. They put feet to their convictions and loved their world with *kalos* power.

THE POWER OF "KALOS" IN OUR DAY . . .

Recently, Nicholas D. Kristoff, a Harvard-Oxford educated Pulitzer Prize winning journalist, editorialized in the *New York Times:*

> Guess what was on the recent cover of the magazine published by Campus Crusade for Christ.
>
> A glowing young couple pledging themselves to sexual abstinence until their wedding night? Nope.

The cover was about poverty in rural Cameroon. And it reflected a broad new trend that is beginning to reshape American foreign policy: America's evangelicals have become the newest internationalists.

The old religious right led by Jerry Falwell and Pat Robertson, trying to battle Satan with school prayers and right-to-life amendments, is on the ropes. It is being succeeded by evangelicals who are using their growing clout to skewer China and North Korea, to support Israel, to fight sexual trafficking in Eastern Europe and slavery in Sudan, and, increasingly, to battle AIDS in Africa.

Evangelicals are usually regarded by snooty, college-educated bicoastal elitists (not that any read this newspaper) as dangerous Neanderthals. But . . . the new internationalists are saving lives in some of the most forgotten parts of the world . . .

I disagree with evangelicals on many issues . . . Yet all in all, we should welcome this new constituency for foreign affairs in Middle America. Just look at AIDS funding: With bleeding-heart evangelicals like Mr. Graham pressing hard, Congressional Republicans are suddenly scrambling to allocate hundreds of millions of dollars in additional money to fight AIDS in Africa. Even Jesse Helms is joining in, and that's pretty much proof of divine intervention. . . .

I've lost my cynicism about evangelical groups partly because I've seen them at work abroad. Early this year, for example, I visited the Philippine island of Basilan, home base of the Abu Sayyaf rebel group. Aid groups have mostly pulled out because of killings and kidnappings, but I found one still busy providing food and medicine even in the most dangerous areas. It's the Christian Children's Fund.[10]

Never underestimate the power of good deeds to catch the attention of a skeptical world.

In the summer of 2001, Houston, Texas, was deluged by rains that caused hundreds of millions of dollars in damage to homes and businesses. The rains began on Friday, and by early Sunday morning it was clear that Houston was buried in a major emergency. The leadership of the Second Baptist Church leveraged the manpower of the church into action. That Sunday they announced the need for people to go into the community to help those struck by the disaster. Major donations filled the offering plates and by early afternoon they had a fleet of trucks, pickups, and vans at their disposal and hundreds of volunteers. They literally emptied the inventories of several major home improvement and hardware stores of Sheetrock, drying fans, and whatever else was necessary to rush to the aid of the needy. They took food to some of the most despairing neighborhoods that were hit the hardest. All in the name of Jesus.

As a friend remarked to me, "The neat thing

was that people didn't just write checks but rolled up their sleeves and got to work."

I asked, "Did many of the flood victions end up coming to your church as a result of the effort?" The reply made me feel like a dunce for asking the question. "We really don't know. We did it because it is what Jesus has called us to do. We leave the results up to Him."

The point is, Houston now knows that it is the followers of Jesus who care when the chips are down.

In fact what makes us distinct from other non-Jesus related charitable activities is that we have a motivation to do good, regardless. We do it to fulfill the love-motivated relationship that we have with Jesus. We serve others *for* Him and *because* of Him, which gives us unusual staying power.

Remember that it was the fact that all the other aid groups had pulled out of the dangerous region in the Philippines except the Christian Children's Fund that caught the attention of Kristof and began to melt his cynicism toward Christians.

The ministry of the English Language Institute in China has been astounding. Although the Chinese leaders are aware that the teachers with ELIC are Christians, they welcome these English teachers to their university campuses. Others who come with the Peace Corps and other secular social agencies rarely fulfill their commitments because of the hardships in living conditions and the culture shock. In fact, they often brought such low morals that the Communist government sees them as a threat to the purity of their culture.

But the persevering attitude and good moral lives of ELIC teachers result in the payoff that not only are the Chinese learning to speak English, they are also encountering Jesus' pure and persevering love flowing from the hearts of their teachers.

But lest you think that the impact of compassion is best felt through massive church programs and faithful international representatives of the King, I need to make it very clear that most often the compassionate power of *kalos* is released every day right in the context of your life and relationships. Sometimes it is manifest in your attitudes as well as your actions.

COMPASSION, THE EVERYDAY VARIETY . . .

Three weeks after 9/11, a friend of mine was in New York City viewing the ground zero landscape. He had brought with him several copies of *The Jesus Film* in different Arabic languages and had been able to pass all of them out except for the video that was in the Egyptian language. On his last day in New York, he prayed that the Lord would lead him to an Egyptian to whom he could give his last video. The day passed without the prayed-for opportunity, and he jumped into a cab for his trip to the airport.

The cab driver was obviously Middle Eastern, and so my friend asked him if people had treated him with hostility since the terrorist attack. The driver let go with expletives describing how he had gone unpaid, how people had taken one look at him and gotten out of his cab, and how hateful most of his riders had been. He angrily expounded on the fact that the 9/11 attack was a Jewish plot. He went on to say that the Jews should be blamed, not the people of his descent.

I will forever love my friend Paul for what he did next. He gently replied to the cab driver, "I am so sorry that people have treated you like that. I'd like to apologize for the way people have treated you." He went on to tell the cabbie that Jesus would never have treated him like that.

The conversation went on in more civil tones, and when they got to the airport the driver climbed out to help Paul with his bags. When Paul asked how much the ride would be, the cabbie said "Nothing. This ride is on me!" Paul insisted but to no avail. When Paul asked the cab driver where he was from, the cabbie said, "Egypt." Paul asked if he spoke Egyptian and the driver said, "Fluently." Paul could hardly believe what he heard and asked him if he would be interested in a video about Jesus in his own language. Eagerly the driver of the cab said "Yes," and took the video from Paul.

You couldn't have asked for a better display of *kalos*-compassion in action!

I like to think that some day I will meet an Egyptian New York cab driver in heaven.

CHAPTER 7

WELCOME ... IN JESUS' NAME

Commitment 4:

Community ... Loving for Jesus

D r. Charles Ware is an African-American. He serves as the founder and president of Crossroads College in Indianapolis. He is a visionary leader whose passion for the cause of Christ is widely recognized. Growing up he came to Jesus out of a life of rugged other-side-of-the tracks experiences. Quite frankly, given the obstacles of his early years he is an unlikely candidate for such success. If it weren't for stubborn grit and a heart of gold, and, most important, God's gracious hand of providence, he would never have made it.

Soon after accepting Christ, Charles felt led to train for the ministry. His pastor friend and mentor recommended that he enroll in a Bible college. The fact that the school was primarily white didn't deter

Charles. He had grown up around Anglos and felt quite comfortable in cross-cultural settings. Besides, knowing that they would all be brothers and sisters in Christ settled what few doubts he had.

Or so he thought.

As a freshman he tried out for the school's soccer team, and after a particularly hot grueling late summer work out another student staring at him said, "Is that how a nigger sweats?"

This comment was the first among several awkward encounters that he experienced as a black student in a "white" Christian school. Incidents that could be written off as naive insensitivity by fellow students could not be excused in the realm of the administration's attitude.

As college students often do, Charles and a co-ed felt their hearts drawn toward each other and soon they were deeply in love.

She was white.

The administration opposed their relationship. He was called on the carpet and pressured to stop dating a white girl. But as I listened to Charles share the story of his early struggles in white church-world, one comment stunned my heart with a sense of sadness and regret.

In one of those meetings geared to encourage Charles to stop dating her, the president's representative said to him, "Your problem is that you need to spend more time with your own people!"

If we understand the teachings of Jesus, the comment is out-of-bounds. Charles *was* spending time with his "own people."

Who Are My Brothers and Sisters . . . ?

Regardless of how one may feel about inter-racial dating, the president's envoy had—knowingly or not—defined belonging and community according to color and culture. In his terms Charles' "own people" were black. Yet in terms of what Jesus taught, Charles' own people are his brothers and sisters in Christ.

One of the radical paradigm shifts Jesus introduced into His world was the notion that true family was no longer based on ancestry but on being born into His family. The radical nature of this shift was scandalous in His day. There was no greater point of loyalty in the ancient world than loyalty to one's brother or sister. In fact, loyalty expressed to your siblings was even more intense than loyalty to parents or spouse.

It was clear from the beginning that one of the purposes of Jesus' mission on earth was to establish a new subculture through which salt and light could be dispensed. This new group would be like family. Family—with its mutual commitments, loyal connectedness, common heritage, and familial mind-set—would now be the way that followers of Jesus should view their relationships.

You would have to be living in the first century to know how scandalous it seemed when Jesus re-defined family. You may recall the time His disciples told Him that His mother and brothers were outside waiting to talk with Him. His reply was offensively revolutionary: "Who are My mother and My brothers?" Then, pointing to His disciples, He said, "Behold My mother and My brothers! For whoever does the will of God, he is My brother and sister and mother" (Mark 3:33–35).

For followers of Jesus, the concept of family would never be the same again.

The early church took the clue. They immediately picked family nomenclature and consistently called each other "brother" and "sister." They acted out their new and strategic identity as any family should. They expressed mutual love, acceptance, and loyalty. They shared goods and resources for one another's benefit. Like a volunteer welfare state, they organized to care for their widows. Old and infirm members found solace and care. The fatherless found mentors, and the bereaved found comfort. They protected one another and marshaled a strong sense of unity against the growing number of enemies that threatened their safety and future.

Gerhard Lohfink observes:

> The type of care—revolutionary in comparison with pagan society—extended in principle to all

members of the community in need of help shows that the use of "brother" and "sister" in Christian communities was not a mere affectation. Care was extended above all to widows, orphans, the elderly and sick, those incapable of working and the unemployed, prisoners and exiles, Christians on a journey and all other members of the church who had fallen into special need. Care was also taken that the poor received a decent burial.

The care of the Christian communities for their unemployed and for those unable to work is worth particular attention. They insisted that all who were able to work did so; they even arranged jobs for them, as much as they were able to. But anyone no longer able to work could be sure of receiving support from the community. They had a system of aiding employment and a network of social security which was unique in the ancient world. It rested both on mutual help and on voluntary contributions gathered primarily at the Sunday Eucharist. Justin (*Apology* 1.67) describes this collection in his well-known depiction of Christian liturgy:

> The wealthy, if they wish, contribute whatever they desire, and the collection is placed in the custody of the president. [With it] he helps the orphans and widows, those who are needy because of sickness or any other reason, and the captives and strangers in our midst.

Lohfink continues:

... Fraternity was thus not an empty word either in
individual communities or in the church as a whole.
"While Christian doctrine appeared utopian and
unrealistic in the eyes of their foes, its practical ap-
plication showed it to be a solid concept for keeping
the economic and social needs of at least the members of the community under control."[1]

Noteworthy to a watching world was the unusual
practice of Christians using their own homes as an
outstretched hand of hospitality that provided strategic way stations for the gospel.

One scholar of early church life notes:

In each city where Christians lived one or more
families made their homes available for the assem-
bly of the community (cf. Acts 12:12; Rom. 16:4, 23;
1 Cor. 16:15, 19; Col. 4:5; Philemon 2). The owners of
the homes (such as Prisca and Aquila) often conducted
vital missionary activity; with self-sacrificing hospitality they made their house both the center of community life and a place of support for Christians
who were traveling. This involved not only hosting
missionaries traveling on behalf of a congregation
(cf. e.g., 2 Cor. 8:23), but also welcoming Christians
underway on their own accord, for example for
business reasons. Extending hospitality to strange

"brothers" played an extraordinary role in the early church. The structure of the new, open family, which transcended its own boundaries in openness to the community, is exemplified in the families of those who placed their homes at its disposal.[2]

This is not to say that the new order didn't face some challenges. The unthinkable notion that Gentiles could be a part of the family caused a feud that nearly destroyed the church in its infancy. But the broadness of His family was so important to God that it took a direct revelation to Peter and a heavy dose of apostolic clout by Paul to clarify the family boundaries. This group of believers in Jesus could not be an exclusive club. It was for all who would find their way to the cross. And that "all" became a big word.

The family included freemen and slaves, men and women, poor and rich, young and old, weak and strong, Jew and Gentile . . . no one was excluded. Everyone held equal standing and had equal access to all the family privileges. This was a huge and compelling statement to a world of isolated and disconnected people. Slaves were obviously people without portfolio. Women were often despised and marginalized. The old were neglected, and the poor looked down on. Not so among these soon to conquer Christians. To demonstrate this new order, the early church practiced foot washing. And it was the elders who washed the feet of all the saints! For early Christians, the ground was so level at the foot of the cross that the apostles often addressed all of the faithful as "saints" and themselves as "servants" (Philippians 1:1).

If you had Jesus in common, you needed no other credential. I am struck by Paul's commentary on the makeup of the church at Corinth. After listing egregious categories of sinners like fornicators, idolaters, the covetous, drunkards, swindlers, thieves, and homosexuals, he says, "Such were some of you; but you were washed, but you were sanctified, but you were justified in the name of our Lord Jesus Christ and in the Spirit of our God" (1 Corinthians 6:11).

That's quite a family!

This broad sense of community in and of itself was one of the most compelling testimonies of the early church. While their world was full of exclusive clubs and guilds, no other organization was so unequivocally open and generously beneficial. The church existed for the benefit of its members.

They had community like no one else and as such they offered their world a welcoming place to belong in Jesus' name.

Historian Will Durant, who is usually amused by or contemptuous toward Christianity, wrote this of early Christianity:

All in all, no more attractive religion has ever been presented to mankind. . . . It offered itself without restrictions to all individuals, classes, and nations; it was not limited to one people, like Judaism, nor to the free-men of one state, like the official cults of Greece and Rome. By making all men heirs of Christ's victory over death, Christianity announced the basic equality of men, and made transiently trivial all differences of earthly degree. To the miserable, maimed, bereaved, disheartened, and humiliated it brought the new virtue of compassion, and an ennobling dignity . . . it brightened their lives with the hope of the coming Kingdom, and of endless happiness beyond the grave. To even the greatest sinners it promised forgiveness, and their full acceptance into the community of the saved. To minds harassed with the insoluble problems of origin and destiny, evil and suffering, it brought a system of divinely revealed doctrine in which the simplest soul could find mental rest . . . into a world sick of brutality, cruelty, oppression, and sexual chaos . . . it brought a new morality of brotherhood, kindliness, decency, and peace. So molded to men's wants, the new faith spread with fluid readiness. Nearly every convert, with the ardor of a revolutionary, made himself an office of propaganda."[5]

WHATEVER HAPPENED TO COMMUNITY . . .

The basic human need to be accepted and affirmed has not changed. Jesus offers to satisfy this longing. He is looking to extend this gracious offer through followers who practice the happy art of sharing in an unusual and enriching love for one another regardless. He needs churches full of people who forgive freely, care sacrificially, mutually protect and provide for one another, and welcome others unconditionally.

Am I missing something or does it seem to you that for the most part people with twisted and sinful lives, with deep personal and spiritual needs, would probably not think of our churches as a place of inclusion, grace, healing, and welcome?

In *What's So Amazing About Grace/* Phil Yancey relates a gripping story that should give all of us pause.

> A prostitute came to [a friend of mine] in wretched straits, homeless, sick, unable to buy food for her two year old daughter. Through sobs and tears, she told me she had been renting out her daughter—two years old!—to men interested in kinky sex. She made more renting out her daughter for an hour than she could earn on her own in a night. She had to do it, she said, to support her own drug habit. I could hardly bear hearing her sordid story. For one thing, it made me legally liable—I'm required to report cases of child abuse. I had no idea what to say to this woman.
>
> At last I asked if she had ever thought of going to a church for help. I will never forget the look of

pure, naive shock that crossed her face. "Church!" she cried. "Why would I ever go there? I was already feeling terrible about myself. They'd just make me feel worse."[4]

Yancey observes, "What struck me about my friend's story is that women much like this prostitute fled toward Jesus, not away from Him. The worse a person felt about herself, the more likely she saw Jesus as a refuge. Has the church lost that gift?"

A couple of Sundays ago while worshiping in church I noticed a well-dressed young woman across the aisle. What caught my attention was the large tattoo that colored her arm. Immediately a slew of thoughts raced across my distracted mind. And—if I can confess—not all real positive. I wondered why and where she had gotten that in the first place. It seemed so incongruous with being in church and participating as a proper worshiper. And sitting right in the front row at that! Did she feel conspicuous and uncomfortable?

Right about then I felt the jab of the Spirit and immediately confessed my sin of denying the very heart and plan of Jesus for the church. I watched her face as she sang words from her heart that obviously held great meaning for her. Had her tattoos been from her previous life without Jesus? Whatever. She was a trophy born into the same family that I was by the same extensive grace that blessed my life. She belonged on the front row. I was the one with the problem. I wondered how many others had the same problem that morning.

I have mentioned before that one of my favorite churches is The Gospel House south of Cleveland, Ohio. It was started by Bob Sepkovich, who at the time had an effective ministry in local and state jail systems. When men who came to the Lord in prison were released, he encouraged them to go to a local church where they could be accountable and involved. Unfortunately, the welcome mat was rarely rolled out for these ex-cons. So he started his own church for these men. Today The Gospel House is a growing, energetic church with people from all walks of life. Executives, former prostitutes, policemen, convicted felons all worship and work for Jesus. It's wonderfully like the early church. It's the way church should be if we are to make a statement about the welcoming arms of Jesus and the breadth of His love and grace.

The last time I attended The Gospel House, a gnarled, thin woman whose body was twisted with disfigured limbs stood in the front row of the choir. Next to her was a lady who was totally blind. What impressed me was the energy with which these two sang and the joy that was so obvious on their faces. It made me wonder why it was that more disabled people weren't active in most churches.

How would you respond if someone confessed to

the church that they had been a practicing homosexual? Having been forgiven by Jesus, they were committed to living a celibate lifestyle, looking to their brothers and sisters for support, prayer, and accountability. Would they be included in your next dinner party? Your small group? At the time for greeting in the service would they be as warmly greeted . . . hugged?

Would everyone from your town feel welcomed by the people in your church? Does your church have a reputation as an outpost of forgiveness and mercy? . . . a reputation for accepting people just as they are? If Jesus accepts us just as we are, then bringing Jesus to our non-Jesus world means that we too must receive people just as they are. Obviously, becoming a part of a "true church" demands that we repent of our sins and seek to live godly lives. But how do we expect people to start the process if they feel that church people are too good for them or too condemning of their lifestyle?

Jesus proved this point, much to the consternation of the Pharisees, when He purposefully engaged those who needed His healing grace. When the religious leader complained that He was eating with tax gatherers and sinners He replied, "It is not those who are healthy who need a physician, but those who are sick; I did not come to call the righteous, but sinners" (Mark 2:16–17).

Sinners are made well in the community of belief. How will that happen if we are not lovingly engaged with them? How will they know that grace and cleansing are theirs through Jesus if all they see is our bent toward properness, standoffishness, pride, prejudice, and fear?

One of the marks of a "true church" is whether or not its membership is made up of people who come from diverse backgrounds. You know that the church has reflected the power of community love when people who have been dredged from the bowels of sin feel loved there. When the disabled are fully accepted. When young people are not judged so much by their faddish ways but for the warm passion of their hearts for Jesus. When people of color and people who are white thrive together in the fellowship. When rich and poor affirm one another with love and acceptance. When women feel safe and children are protected.

Francis Schaeffer makes the point with these penetrating words: "Christians have not always presented a pretty picture to the world. Too often they have failed to show the beauty of love, the beauty of Christ, the holiness of God. And the world has turned away. Is there no way to make the world look again—this time at true Christianity? Must Christians continue to stand with arms folded, going on in their old sweet ways, presenting to men a tarnished image of God—a shattered body of Christ?"[5]

THE LAST COMMAND . . .

I'm reminded of the words of Jesus when He said to His disciples, "By this all men will know that you are My disciples, if you have love one for another" (John 13:35). Good words for all of us who have wrongly thought that others will know we belong to Jesus because we don't "dance, smoke, chew, or go with girls that do." Our real point of identity, the authentic mark of belongingness to Jesus is how we treat one another. Christ intends that we treat each other with *agape* love, an intentional, unconditional, committed concern for one another's welfare. A concern that gets busy with actions that prove the love we claim to possess.

This "Jesus-type" of love is intended to be without limits. If He died to love us, we must love to the death if necessary. Which leaves us without excuse in terms of the good that we do for one another. If He sacrificed, so must we. If His love extended to all mankind, regardless, so must ours. If He loved His enemies, so must we. If He was patient and kind in spite of misunderstanding and unfair criticism, we must be also. If He loved the unlovable, so must we.

Granted, you don't get to choose your siblings in your earthly family nor do you get to choose them in your spiritual family—Jesus does the choosing. So regardless of who your brother is and who your sister

happens to be, you have one front-line responsibility
—*to love them as Jesus loved you.*

I am taken with the thought that Jesus taught us
the key to abiding in Him was to keep His commandments. And the command He was talking about is our
requirement to love one another. He said, "If you keep
My commandments, you will abide in My love. . . .
These things I have spoken to you so that My joy may
be in you, and that your joy be made full. This is My
commandment, that you love one another, just as I
have loved you" (John 15:10–12). Don't miss it. Failing to
extend love to our brothers and sisters significantly injures our own fellowship with Jesus. When we love one
another, we abide in Him. He takes great joy in us
when we love one another. Our joy is the fullest when
we, in obedience to Him, love each other.

Church Is No Longer About Me . . .

Are there any widows in your church? Fatherless
children? Single moms? Single dads? Older people?
Lonely hearts? People hurt by the brutal events of
life? Couples who need to know how to rear their
children? People who are hospitalized without family
in the area? Individuals who have been marginalized by others in your church?

This list is just a start.

What do you have in the toolbox of your resources

that can extend the love of Jesus to a person in need? What can you do to be a friend at church?

Do you have money, time, energy, skills, a listening ear, a praying heart, a loving touch, a smile, a friendly hello, a "How are you?", a spiritual gift in action, the capacity for hospitality? Can you deliver a warm dinner to a family in need?

I know a church that goes each autumn to the elderly in their fellowship to wash their windows and change the screens to storms.

Another church fixes cars for single moms, widows, and the elderly who otherwise would not be able to pay for the maintainance of their vehicles.

A church in Texas takes single parents away on long weekend vacations with child-care provided just to bring a season of relief to an otherwise over-stressed life.

There are countless churches who regularly do exchange services with ethnic churches in their town to demonstrate that "community" stretches across church lines and includes all true followers of Jesus regardless of where they worship.

What does your church do to express to your non-Jesus community the limitless, positive value of being a part of the best family in the whole world? In fact, what have you done lately to make this part of Jesus' agenda a reality in your own life?

CHAPTER 8

THE CENTRALITY OF JESUS

Commitment 5:

Consecration...Living for Jesus

There are only a few great ballparks left in America. In fact, just two. Fenway Park in Boston and Wrigley Field in Chicago. As wonderful as the ambiance of these get-close-to-the-field-take-me-out-to-the-ball-game stadiums may be, there is one problem. Some of the seats are directly behind a post. Those unfortunate enough to occupy the seats have an obstructed view. They are in the ballpark and can hear the action but can't quite see the whole game.

Tragically, that's often the way we experience our life in Christ: There are lots of distractions and disappointments that get in the way of making Him the all-compelling center of our existence. And, if He is not the consuming center of our lives, there is little hope of taking Him into our world.

SACRED DISTRACTIONS

I was sitting in a men's meeting when the speaker asked us to think of the denomination to which we belonged. That was easy for me. I was born and bred a Baptist and, in fact, I am the son and grandson of Baptist preachers. And, while I have long ago realized that Baptists aren't the only ones going to heaven, growing up Baptist indelibly pressed its mark into my spiritual identity, and to this day my upbringing has blessed me with many valuable perspectives in my walk with Christ.

The speaker asked all of us to shout out our denominational identity. It sounded like a Pentecostal revival without an interpreter. Then he asked us to call out the name *Jesus*. The mass celebration of unintelligible noise as men spoke, shouted, cheered, and whistled for their own point of view now paled in comparison to the beauty and strength of the proclamation of His name alone.

The demonstration of the centrality of Jesus brought me great joy and satisfaction.

If our true identity is that we are first and foremost followers of Jesus, shouldn't it be the first thing on our mind, the first thing on our list? Sometimes I am in groups where John Calvin is quoted more often and with more authority than Jesus or the apostles. To his credit, John Calvin would be embarrassed.

A prevalent obstruction to the centrality and supremacy of Jesus is our preoccupation with ourselves. Why do we keep embarrassing ourselves and Jesus by living lives that are consumed with ourselves— my preferences, my style, my perspectives, my plans?

If we are followers of Jesus, it is supposed to be all about *Him*.

And isn't it interesting that where Jesus should be the most visible—at church—He is often obscured by the misplaced priority of our own expectations and preferences. How often have you heard someone grumpily complain, "Well, I didn't get anything at all out of the sermon this morning"? What a misguided perspective! Maybe the sermon wasn't for them. Maybe it was for some needy soul at the other end of the pew. Or was it the music that we didn't like or the dress that a worship leader was wearing?

Was Jesus proclaimed and worshiped? That is the real issue. In light of the overarching issue of becoming a devoted follower and engaging our world with salt and light, if church is all about us, we inevitably end up sounding petty and small.

But it's not just Sunday.

It's easy to be distracted on Monday as well when we go to our jobs or rush the kids off to school and run those forever and present errands. Rarely do you find followers who have advanced from the backwaters of self-interest to view their career, family, and friendships in the light of the preeminence of Jesus and the calling that we be salt and light in our world. Life is often about how much money we can make, how we can position ourselves for that long-sought-after promotion, how we are treated by colleagues and friends, if we will have time for golf, and whether we have the right clothes to wear. We need to remember what Jesus taught His distracted disciples when He said, "Seek first His kingdom and His righteousness, and all these things shall be added to you" (Matthew 6:33).

Some of us deal with deep obstructional problems. It may be hard to see Jesus clearly if your dad, who abused you as a child, is now a leader in the church. Or perhaps your pastor's attitude and lifestyle are not worthy of respect. Granted, these deep, unsettling experiences have vast ramifications and often defy simple answers. We must remind ourselves that Jesus also despises these kinds of destructive behaviors. His perfect love welcomes you to come out from behind the pain of your disillusionment and disappointment in order to see His face and experience His healing touch.

The wonderful news is that Jesus welcomes you to an unobstructed field box seat. Look for Him. When you see Him in all His fullness the usual obstructions fall into perspective. As Peter says, "He who believes in Him will not be disappointed" (1 Peter 2:6).

Follow Me! . . .

Becoming a devoted follower is step one in making Jesus central in your life. Getting a grip on what followership means is critical if we are going to be effective in living for Jesus in our non-Jesus world. Here are some applications that will help you bring the issue of following Jesus into sharper focus. In one of the initial encounters that Jesus had with soon to be followers, Matthew tells us:

> *As Jesus was walking beside the Sea of Galilee, he saw two brothers, Simon called Peter and his brother Andrew. They were casting a net into the lake, for they were fishermen. "Come, follow me," Jesus said, "and I will make you fishers of men." At once they left their nets and followed him.*
>
> *Going on from there, he saw two other brothers, James son of Zebedee and his brother John. They were in a boat with their father Zebedee, preparing their nets. Jesus called them, and immediately they left the boat and their father and followed him.* (Matthew 4:18–22 NIV)

From this text we learn that there are three dynamics to authentic followership.

Imitation of Him . . .

The word Jesus used when He said, "Follow me," has two descriptive meanings in the Greek. The first meaning is to *replicate* Jesus in attitude and action. In Christ's day the term *follower* referred to people who had such a deep longing for God that they would attach themselves to the local rabbi, who was the closest connection they could find to God. In some cases, young men would actually sacrifice their entire careers in order to live with and serve at the feet of a respected rabbi. Because they spent so much time with the rabbi they revered, they often started talking like him, using the same words he did, and gesturing and thinking as he did. In fact, followers were often identified with the rabbi they served because they acted and responded to life in the same way he did.

Jesus, the Rabbi of our souls, is the only way to get our longing for God satisfied. The more we spend time with Him, serve Him, sit at His feet, and surrender to Him, the more we become like Him. Early followers did this so effectively that a noticing world gave them the name *Christians*.

PASSIONATE PURSUIT OF HIM . . .

The second nuance of the word *follow* means to pursue the one you are following. What is the pursuit of your life? What are your dreams? What do you want to become? What occupies your heart and interests?

To follow Him means that your desires, dreams, and goals are formed by Jesus and what He wishes for your life. It is about getting closer and closer to Him with every decision, every desire, and every dream. This concept of what it means to follow Christ is revolutionary in its implications. Although boundaries of good living and good doctrine are important, true Christianity places Jesus at the center of life and compels us to move toward Him.

Most of us began this journey when we accepted Him. Regrettably, at some point we feel that we are close enough to Him and allow ourselves to move into orbit around Him. It's easy to feel quite good about ourselves and where we are in comparison to others whose orbits are further away from Him.

Not so with true followers. True followers stay in hot pursuit of Jesus, who promised that He is a rewarder of them that diligently seek Him. As we become more like Him and passionately pursue Him, it becomes apparent that He is leading us to the needs of people who are lost in their non-Jesus world. It's no wonder that Jesus said to His disciples, "Follow Me, and I will make you fishers of men" (Matthew 4:19).

In the Way with Him . . .

Third, when Matthew tells us that the disciples dropped their nets and followed Jesus, he used a different word for following that is equally descriptive. It means "to be found in the way" with the one you are following. It is the "ways" of Jesus that indelibly mark the life of a follower. Like Jesus, followers forgive cruelty and injustice, care for the needy and the poor, and use their resources to love their neighbors and care for the "one anothers" in their community of belief. Followers live with eternity in mind. They are true to their word, and they use the money according to kingdom purposes. This is but a sampling of what it means to be found in the Way with Him.

Given these revolutionary characteristics of followers, it's easy to see why true followers make a difference in their non-Jesus world

But, in order to make a difference, like those first followers, we must drop our nets to follow Him. What are the nets that distract you from being a devoted follower? What are the issues you cling to that keep Jesus from being central in your life? What obstructions are you still hiding behind?

Followers are netless believers!

If we are genuinely committed to following Jesus, the path behind us will be littered with the nets we have refused to carry and our eyes will be fixed on Jesus, who leads us on the greatest adventure in life . . . following Him.

SOME HONEST REFLECTION . . .

Becoming an authentic follower necessitates a journey into your interior—a journey that leads to a short list of issues that need to be resolved.

Has there ever been a time when Jesus was so valued in your life that you were willing to stick up for Him, regardless?

Are you ready to speak up for Jesus in clear, humble, and compassionate tones?

Can you think of any actions and attitudes that salt your world with His joy and purifying, preserving presence through you?

In what ways are you ready to engage your world with His love?

When was the last time you started your day with the resolve to do something special to light up the lives of others with the compelling power of *kalos*?

What was the last *kalos* deed you blessed your world with?

In what ways is your love for fellow followers intentional, unconditional, and compellingly effective?

Is Jesus at the center of your life, and are you actively pursuing Him?

Has anyone noticed?

GETTING IT ALL TOGETHER . . .

During the public games in February A.D. 155, excited crowds began calling for the death of Polycarp, bishop of the city of Smyrna. "Away with the Atheists!" they shouted, "Let Polycarp be sought out!"[1] His location was betrayed by a young girl who had been tortured, and soldiers came for him. While in the hands of his captors, he insisted that they be given a meal and provided with all they wished while he spent one last hour in prayer. Polycarp had lived such a good and noble life that even the captain of the guard didn't wish to see him die. On the brief journey back to the city, the captain pled with the old man: "What harm is there in saying, Lord Caesar, and in sacrificing, and so make sure of safety?"[1]

Upon Polycarp's arrival at the arena, the proconsul gave him the choice of cursing the name of Christ and making sacrifice to Caesar, or death. The bishop's response has rung down through the centuries as a model for faithful followers. He replied, "Eighty and six years have I served Him, and He never did me any injury: how then can I blaspheme my King and my Savior?"

Threatened with death at the stake, Polycarp then helped put things in perspective for his enemies: "Thou threatenest me with fire which burneth for an hour, and after a little is extinguished, but art ignorant of the fire of the coming judgment and of eternal punishment, reserved for the ungodly." In spite of the appeals of even the persecutors, he remained immovable. He was loosely bound at the stake and burned. In life, his greatest pursuit had been Christ, even to the point of death. As the flames rose around him he prayed his final prayer. Part of it says, "I give Thee thanks that Thou hast counted me worthy of this day and this hour, that I should have a part in the number of Thy martyrs, in the cup of thy Christ, to the resurrection of eternal life, both of soul and body, through the incorruption [imparted] by the Holy Ghost."

In a sense, Polycarp models all we have been learning. He lived life so well that even his enemies begged him to recant. He *kalosed* his enemies by feeding the soldiers who came to take him to his death. He resolutely stayed faithful to Jesus. And having shown up for Jesus in such spectacular ways, he seized the opportunity to articulately speak up for Jesus with unmistakable clarity all the way to his dying prayer.

LETTING JESUS IN . . .

One of the great depictions of Jesus in the history of art was painted by William Holman Hunt. In his painting *The Light of the World,* he portrays Jesus knocking at a door. On the frame of the picture he had etched the verse from Revelation 3:20, written to followers in the ancient city of Laodecia. "Behold, I stand at the door and knock; if anyone hears My voice and opens the door, I will come in to him and will dine with him, and he with Me."

The striking thing about Holman's picture is that Jesus is standing outside the door, holding a lamp in His hand. The imagery is clear. If Jesus is on the outside of your life, so is His light. There is no hope of lighting the world around you until you let Him in to light your world.

When Jesus wrote the letter to the Laodecian church, He pictured Himself on the outside of their heart's door because in their affluence and self-made lives they didn't think they needed Him. In a very real sense they had constructed their world as a non-Jesus world. And, strange as it seems, many of us have done the same thing. We feel we have all we need without Him.

No doubt the Laodecians were glad to have Him as Savior, attend His church, even serve on committees and boards. But until they needed Him at death's door, they would do life much as they pleased. And so an excluded Jesus stood at the door of their hearts seeking to come in. He is standing at your heart's door seeking to come in with the light for your world gripped firmly in His hand. If you're arguing that Jesus is already "in you," then you have missed the point. He can be resident somewhere in the territory of your life without being the all-controlling center of your heart. He seeks to set up His throne in your heart where decisions, dreams, plans, and intentions are forged.

Surrendering fully to Jesus is the key to beginning a life that effectively impacts your world for Him.

LET JESUS PAY . . .

Most often, I find that the opportunities to engage my world for Jesus are rather unspectacular, somewhat routine encounters that God turns into strategic moments.

The other day I had completed my morning "run-walk" along Lake Michigan and stopped two blocks away from home to pick up a Starbucks coffee. As I stood in line, the guy in front of me was having a tense discussion with the clerk about the fact that he only had a fifty-dollar bill with which to buy the copy of *The New York Times* he was holding in his hand. The clerk was doing his best to remain pleasant as he explained that they didn't have that much change that early in the morning. As the conversation grew more heated, I could see that the man with the newspaper was running out of options, so I threw a dollar down on the counter and said, "I'll pay for it!"

Gratefully, the proud new owner of the newspaper thanked me profusely and jokingly commented, "All I have is yours!" as he walked away. Unfortunately it was apparent that "all I have" didn't include the fifty-dollar bill! But what the clerk was about to say to me was worth it all. As he handed me my change and my goods, he looked at me and said, "What you did was a really nice thing. The world would be a better place if more people would be like you." Quite frankly I was taken back by his comment. He quickly turned to help the next customer as I mumbled some kind of deferring response and headed home.

I wasn't half a block away when I thought of what I could have said. I could have responded, "Actually the world would be a better place if we were all more like Jesus. He's the one who taught me how to do that. He gave everything He had to me!"

I recalled the time, many years ago now, that my Hebrew professor had been given too much change at the bank. As he realized that the teller had overpaid him, he said to her, "You have given me more than I should have." She recounted the money and said, "My, you're an honest man!" To which he replied, "It's not that I'm an honest man; it is that Jesus has changed my life!"

Oh to be so quick!

I felt sick! I had shown up for Jesus but hadn't been prepared enough in my heart to speak up for Jesus.

I wondered if I should go back to tell him, but the shop was already crowded with people waiting in line. I didn't think it would be a lot like Jesus to butt in line and make a "religious" statement for everyone to hear.

Perhaps the clerk wasn't ready to hear about Jesus. Sometimes it's OK simply to bless our world with the presence of Jesus through us. And I'm convinced that there are times when the Spirit purposely withholds the words . . . when for reasons best known to Him, words would not be productive.

Yet I always want to be ready to speak up for Jesus. So I'm praying that the Lord will keep the matter of speaking up for Him more clearly on my mind and that He will give me another opportunity to do so soon.

My only consolation that morning was the fact that I was wearing my old Moody Bible Institute cap.

I hope he noticed!

Actually, I hope he gets around a lot of us and notices! Perhaps someday he will want to know why the world is a better place because followers of Jesus have crossed his path.

Lighting the Night . . .

For centuries God has sought to validate the reality of His existence and the truth of His claims through bold acts of incontrovertible proof lived out through the lives of His people. In the midst of the multiple gods of the Caananites, Israel proved that their God was singularly superior by walking through parted seas and by remarkable military conquests against the greatest of odds.

But most significant, God has often chosen the unlikeliest of people to clinch the truth that He is a God above all gods and that there is no other god like Him. From a stuttering Moses, who would be used to demonstrate his God's superiority over the gods of Egypt; to Elijah, who would shame the prophets of Baal; to the blind, lame, and sick, who by the touch of Jesus told a watching world that Jesus was the only true and living God.

And now it's your turn. Touched by Jesus, you are commissioned to use your life to bless an often hostile, non-Jesus world with the undeniable reality of the power and presence of His love.

This is our day . . . we are His salt and light . . . it is our destiny and privilege!

Don't miss the opportunity!

Carpe diem!

Therefore God exalted him to the highest place
and gave him the name that is above every name,

that at the name of Jesus every knee should bow,
in heaven and on earth and under the earth,

and every tonue confess that Jesus Christ is Lord,
to the glory of God the Father.

Philippians 2:9-11

NOTES

Chapter 1: Breakfast Without Jesus

1. Diane Eck, *A New Religious America: How a "Christian Country" Has Become the World's Most Religiously Diverse Nation* (San Francisco: Harper, 2002).

2. Thomas Freidman, *The New York Times*, 27 November 2001.

3. Bishop C. Joseph Sprague, *Chicago Tribune*, Associated Press, 19 November 1991.

4. Gene Edward Veith, "The New Multi-Faith Religion: Faithful Christians Better Be Ready to Become Unpopular," *World Magazine*, 15 December 2001, Volume 16, Number 48.

5. Betsy Wright, "These Defenders of the Faith Come Off Looking Offensive," *The Virginian-Pilot*, 8 December 2001, Final Edition, E3.

Chapter 2: Déjà Vu All Over Again

1. Peter Berger, *A Rumor of Angels: Modern Society and the Rediscovery of the Supernatural* (New York: Doubleday, 1969, 1990).

2. Robert Wilken, *The Christians as Romans Saw Them* (New Haven: Yale Univ. Press, 1984), 105.

3. C. S. Lewis, *The Last Battle,* book 7 of *The Tales of Narnia* (New York: Collier Books, 1970), 31–32.

4. Ibid, 132–33.

5. Will Durant, *Caesar and Christ* (New York: Simon and Schuster, 1944), 602.

Chapter 3: Terms of Engagement

1. Interview, Lisa Beamer and Larry King, *Larry King Live!* 18 September 2001.

2. In John MacArthur, *Matthew 1–7,* New Testament Commentary (Chicago: Moody, 1985), 242.

3. H. L. Mencken, *The Minority Report: H. L. Mencken's Notebooks* (New York: Knopf, 1956), no. 309.

4. Speech of Mother Teresa of Calcutta to the National Prayer Breakfast, Washington, D.C., 3 February 1994. This text was accessed at www.priestsforlife.org in the subsection Brochures.

5. Philo, *De Speciabilus Legitus,* 2:253, quoted in N. T. Wright, *The Challenge of Jesus* (London: SPCA, 2000), 379.

6. N. T. Wright, *The Challenge of Jesus,* 38.

Chapter 4: Jesus in the No-Spin Zone

1. Colin Nicholl,"The Nativity Is a Scandal and Should Remain One," *The Times,* 24 December 2001, 10. Originally printed in *The Times* and used by their permission and by permission of Colin Nicholl.

2. E. R. Dodds, *Pagan and Christian in an Age of Anxiety: Some Aspects of Religious Experience from Marcus Aurelius to Constantine* (Cambridge: Cambridge Univ. Press, 1965), quoted in Joseph H. Hellerman, *The Ancient Church as Family* (Minneapolis: Fortress, 2001), 2.

3. Douglas Coupland, *Life After God* (New York: Pocket, 1994), 359.

Chapter 5: Jesus in the Spotlight

1. Charles Colson, "Reaching the Pagan Mind," *Christianity Today*, 9 November 1992, 112, quoted in Gene Edward Veith Jr., *Postmodern Times: A Christian Guide to Contemporary Thought and Culture* (Wheaton, Ill.: Crossway, 1994), 15–16.

2. David McCullough, *Truman* (New York: Simon & Schuster, 1992), 185.

3. Ibid.

4. Vincent Carroll and David Shiflett, *Christianity on Trial: Arguments Against Anti-Religious Bigotry* (San Francisco: Encounter, 2001), 139.

5. Carl F. Henry, *Twilight of a Great Civilisation: The Drift Toward Neo-Paganism,* (Wheaton, IL: Crossway, 1988), 18–19.

Chapter 6: Jesus to the Needy

1. See discussion in Joseph H. Hellerman, *The Ancient Church as Family* (Minneapolis: Fortress, 2001).

2. MacMullen, Ramsay, *Christianizing the Roman Empire: A.D. 100–400* (New Haven: Yale Univ. Press, 1986), 110; cited in Hellerman, *The Ancient Church as Family*, 232, n 3.

3. Hellerman, *The Ancient Church as Family*, 232, n. 3.

4. E. R. Dodds, *Pagan and Christian in an Age of Anxiety: Some Aspects of Religious Experience from Marcus Aurelius to Constantine* (Cambridge: Cambridge Univ. Press, 1965), quoted in Joseph H. Hellerman, *The Ancient Church as Family* (Minneapolis: Fortress, 2001), 3.

5. Hellerman, *The Ancient Church as Family.*

6. Ibid.

7. Vincent Carroll, and David Shiflett, *Christianity on Trial: Arguments Against Anti-Religious Bigotry* (Encounter, 2001), 142.

8. Carroll and Shiflett, *Christianity on Trial*, 146.

9. Ibid., 7.

10. Nicholas D. Kristof, "Following God Abroad," *The New York Times*, 21 May 2002.

Chapter 7: Welcome . . . in Jesus' Name

1. Gerald Lohfink, *Jesus and Community: The Social Dimension of Christian Faith*, translated by John P. Galvin (Philadelphia: Fortress, 1984), 155–56; "While Christian doctrine . . ." is from H.J. Drexhage, "Wirtschaft und Handel in den frühchristlichen Gemeinden (1.–3. Jh. n. Chr.)." *RömischeQuartalschrift* 76 (1981): 1–72. This book is a translation of *Wie hat Jesus Gemeinde Gewoll?* by Gerhard Lohfink, copyright 1982 by Herder Verlag, Freiburg/Basel/Vienna.

2. Ibid., 107-8.

3. Will Durant, *Caesar and Christ* (New York: Simon & Schuster, 1944), 602.

4. Phil Yancey, *What's So Amazing About Grace?* (Grand Rapids: Zondervan, 1997), 11. This story originally appeared in Yancey's book *The Jesus I Never Knew*.

5. Francis Schaeffer, *The Mark of the Christian* (Downers Grove, Ill.: InterVarsity, 1970), foreward.

Chapter 8: The Centrality of Jesus

1. The account of Polycarp's martyrdom, and particularly Polycarp's statements, is taken from *The Encyclical Epistle of the Church at Smyrna Concerning the Martyrdom of the Holy Polycarp*, quoted in John MacArthur, *Revelation 1-11*, The New Testament Commentary (Chicago: Moody, 1999), 72-75. See also William Barclay, editor and translator, *The Daily Study Bible, The Revelation of John*, vol. 1 (Philadelphia: Westminster), 94.

JOSEPH M. STOWELL is the seventh president of the Moody Bible Institute of Chicago, a popular conference speaker, and the voice of the award-winning radio program Proclaim! He has written more than ten books, including *The Weight of Your Words, Eternity, Far From Home, Simply Jesus,* and *Strength for the Journey.* He and his wife, Martie, live in Chicago and are the parents of three grown children and seven grandchildren.

SINCE 1894, Moody Publishers has been dedicated to equip and motivate people to advance the cause of Christ by publishing evangelical Christian literature and other media for all ages, around the world. Because we are a ministry of the Moody Bible Institute of Chicago, a portion of the proceeds from the sale of this book go to train the next generation of Christian leaders.

If we may serve you in any way in your spiritual journey toward understanding Christ and the Christian life, please contact us at www.moodypublishers.com.

"All Scripture is God-breathed and is useful for teaching, rebuking, correcting and training in righteousness, so that the man of God may be thoroughly equipped for every good work."

—2 TIMOTHY 3:16, 17

MOODY
PUBLISHERS

THE NAME YOU CAN TRUST®